TALK TO ME IN KOREAN
LEVEL 10

The Final Step in Talk To Me In Korean's
Essential Korean Curriculum

This book is based on a series of published lessons, divided into ten levels, which are currently available at https://talktomeinkorean.com

TALK TO ME IN KOREAN
- LEVEL 10 -

Talk To Me In Korean - Level 10

1판 1쇄 • 1st edition published	2021. 8. 2
1판 4쇄 • 4th edition published	2025. 1. 6

집필 • Written by	Talk To Me In Korean 연구진 (선현우 Hyunwoo Sun, 선경화 Kyung-hwa Sun, 석다혜 Dahye Seok, 김은희 Eunhee Kim)
프로젝트 매니징 • Project managed by	선경화 Kyung-hwa Sun
교정 및 교열 • Proofread by	서교원 Kyowon Seo
번역 감수 • Translation Reviewed by	김현숙 Annie Kim
디자인 • Designed by	선윤아 Yoona Sun
삽화 • Illustrations by	김경해 Kyounghae Kim
녹음 • Voice Recordings by	선현우 Hyunwoo Sun, 최경은 Kyeong-eun Choi, 석다혜 Dahye Seok
펴낸곳 • Published by	롱테일북스 Longtail Books
펴낸이 • Publisher	이수영 Su Young Lee
편집 • Copy-edited by	김보경 Florence Kim
주소 • Address	04033 서울특별시 마포구 양화로 113, 3층(서교동, 순흥빌딩)
	3rd Floor, 113 Yanghwa-ro, Mapo-gu, Seoul, KOREA
이메일 • E-mail	editor@ltinc.net
ISBN	979-11-91343-18-2 14710

*이 교재의 내용을 사전 허가 없이 전재하거나 복제할 경우 법적인 제재를 받게 됨을 알려 드립니다.

*잘못된 책은 구입하신 서점이나 본사에서 교환해 드립니다.

*정가는 13,000원입니다. 단, 판매 지역과 환율 변동 및 기타 상황에 따라 변경될 수 있습니다.

TTMIK - TALK TO ME IN KOREAN

MESSAGE
FROM
THE AUTHOR

There are billions of bilingual people in the world, and you often see some who switch seemingly effortlessly between two or more languages. So naturally, when you struggle sometimes with learning Korean, you may think that you are not talented or that you are learning too slowly. But the truth is, learning a new language is no easy feat and requires a lot of hard work and dedication! And after many months and possibly years of consistent effort, you are finally here. You have reached Level 10, the grand finale of Talk To Me In Korean's essential Korean curriculum! Congratulations on coming this far and not giving up.

Since you have made it this far, you know exactly what to do with this book – use it to learn even more new expressions and words to add to your Korean knowledge. As usual, you will find useful expressions and grammar points in this book that will help you speak Korean even more fluently. Enjoy! And remember that Level 10 is not the end, but just the conclusion of one big chapter of your Korean learning journey. You will continue learning more and more new words and phrases, acquire cultural knowledge, and discover new real-life usages of words you already know. Learning a new language is a life-long process of continuous improvement, and you are on the right track. Keep going!

여러분, 중간에 포기하지 않고 마지막 레벨인 10까지 오신 것을 정말 축하드립니다. 하지만 여기서 끝이 아니에요. 멈추지 않고 계속 공부하시면 하고 싶은 말을 모두 한국어로 표현할 수 있게 되실 거예요. 지금까지 해 오신 것처럼만 하시면 됩니다. 다양한 문화적 지식은 그 과정에서 자연스럽게 쌓일 거예요. 앞으로도 한국어 공부 계속 즐겁게 하시기를 바랄게요!

TABLE OF
CONTENTS

LESSON **1**

Advanced Idiomatic Expressions 12

> # 얼굴 (Face)

This is an Advanced Idiomatic Expressions lesson related to 얼굴, face. In order to fully understand and use the expressions introduced in this series, it is essential that you understand the grammatical structure of the sentences. When you come across a grammar point that you are unfamiliar with, please go back and review the related TTMIK lessons.

Keyword: **얼굴** = face

I. **얼굴이 낯이 익다** = to look familiar

▷ **낯이 익다** = to be familiar with

Technically speaking, 얼굴 and 낯 both refer to the same thing, which is "one's face". However, 얼굴 is used in everyday speech, whereas 낯 is used more often as part of the idiomatic expressions "낯이 익다 (= to be familiar)" and "낯설다 (= to be unfamiliar)". When you see someone who looks familiar or who you feel like you have met before, you can say, "얼굴이 낯이 익어요."

8

Ex)

저 사람 제가 어디서 봤죠? 얼굴이 낯이 익어요.

= Where have I seen that person? He looks familiar.

2. 어디서 많이 본 얼굴이다 = to look familiar

▷ 어디서 = somewhere

Here, 어디서 does not mean "where", but actually "somewhere". The expression can be literally translated as "it is a face that I have seen a lot somewhere", and has the same meaning as the first expression, 얼굴이 낯이 익다.

Ex)

어디서 많이 본 얼굴인데 누군지 모르겠어요.

= She looks quite familiar, but I do not know who she is.

Track
01

3. 얼굴이 까맣게 타다 = to have a tan (on one's face)

▷ 까맣게 = in black

▷ 타다 = to be burned

Although getting a tan and getting sunburned are two different things, in Korean, 타다 (to be burned) usually refers to getting a suntan. To make the difference between the two clear, sometimes people will say "까맣게 타다 (= to be burned black)" to talk about a suntan, and "빨갛게 타다 (= to be burned red)" or "빨갛게 익다 (= to be cooked red)" to talk about a sunburn.

Ex)

휴가 다녀왔어요? 얼굴이 까맣게 탔네요.

= Were you on a vacation? Your face is tanned.

9

4. **걱정스러운 얼굴을 하고 있다** = to look worried

  ▷ 걱정스러운 = worried, concerned

Translated literally, this expression means "to be doing/wearing a worried face". This expression can be used when you want to emphasize the fact that someone seems worried, regardless of whether or not they are actually worried.

Ex)

왜 그렇게 걱정스러운 얼굴을 하고 앉아 있어요?

= Why are you sitting there looking all worried?

5. **얼굴에 쓰여 있다** = to be written all over one's face

  ▷ 쓰여 있다 = to be written

When you say that something is written on a person's face, it means that you can read their thoughts or emotions by looking at them.

Ex)

거짓말이라고 얼굴에 다 쓰여 있어요.

= I know it is a lie. It is written all over your face.

6. **얼굴을 붉히다** = to blush; to be angry

  ▷ 붉히다 = to make something turn red

When your face turns red (in other words, when blood rushes to your face), it could be because you are embarrassed and are blushing, or because you are upset.

Ex)

이건 그렇게 얼굴 붉힐 일이 아니에요.

= This is not something to be mad about like that.

7. 얼굴만 내밀다 = to just say "hi"

▷ 내밀다 = to stick out

Just like when you "pop your head in/out", when you "stick your face out/in" to greet someone briefly, you are not interacting much with the person. When you stop by a place very briefly and just say "hi", you can say 얼굴만 내밀다 or 얼굴만 비치다. 비치다 describes literally how light or color is reflected on something.

Track
01

Ex)

가기 싫어도 잠깐 얼굴만 내밀고 와요.

= Even if you do not want to go, just stop in and say "hi".

8. 아는 얼굴이 없다 = to not know anyone (in a certain place)

Translated literally, this phrase means "there is no face I know", so the actual meaning is to "not know anyone in a certain place". You can say this when you visit a place after a long absence or when you go to a gathering of new people for the first time.

Ex)

오랜만에 왔더니 아는 얼굴이 별로 없네요.

= Since I have come back after quite a long while, there are not many people that I know.

11

9. 모르는 얼굴들이 많다 = there are a lot of people one does not know

Similar to 아는 얼굴이 없다, when you say that there are a lot of faces that you do not know, it means that most of the people with you in a certain place or group are strangers.

Ex)
오랜만에 왔더니 모르는 얼굴들이 많네요.
= It has been a while since I have been here, and now there are a lot of people who I do not know.

10. 얼굴이 좋아 보이다 = to look great, healthy

Track 01

When you say "your face looks good", it does not mean that someone is good-looking, but rather that someone looks healthier than they did before, or that someone has gained some (but not too much) healthy weight.

Ex)
오랜만이에요. 전보다 얼굴이 좋아 보이네요.
= Long time no see. You look healthy!

11. 무슨 얼굴로 = how can you not be ashamed to...
▷ 무슨 = what kind of

When you have done something bad or something that you should be ashamed of, you might not want to see other people. Therefore, when you have done something bad to someone, but you still have the nerve to show your face, others might say, "How can you

12

show your face?" This has the implied meaning of, "How can you not be ashamed to do this?"

Ex)

여기를 무슨 얼굴로 찾아왔어요?

= How can you not be ashamed to visit me here?

12. 얼굴에 철판을 깔다 = to be shameless

▷ 철판 = steel plate

▷ 깔다 = to lay; to pave

Track 01

When someone is shamelessly asking for a favor or voicing a strong opinion, or when someone does not have a sense of guilt about something they did, you can say that their face is "thick" in Korean (얼굴이 두껍다). An exaggeration of this expression is 얼굴에 철판을 깔다, which means "to have a layer of steel on one's face".

Ex)

저 사람은 얼굴에 철판 깔았나 봐요. 어떻게 여기를 또 오지?

= That person is really shameless. How can he come here again?

13

Sample Dialogue

동근: 두루 씨, 왜 그렇게 걱정스러운 얼굴을 하고 있어요? 무슨 일 있어요?

두루: 아니요. 아무 일도 없어요.

동근: 무슨 일 있다고 얼굴에 다 쓰여 있는데요?

두루: 사실 미국에 있는 가족들이 걱정돼서요. 오랫동안 미국에 못 갔잖아요.

동근: 다들 잘 계실 거예요. 너무 걱정하지 마세요.

Dong-geun: Duru, why are you looking so worried? What's wrong?

Duru: It's nothing.

Dong-geun: It's written all over your face that something's wrong.

Duru: Actually, I'm worried about my family in the States. I haven't been able to go to the States for a long time, as you know.

Dong-geun: I'm sure they're doing well. Don't worry too much.

The Final Step in Talk To Me In Korean's

🖊 Exercises for Lesson *1*

Fill in the blanks with the appropriate idioms with **얼굴** *from the lesson.*

1. (   )

  = to be shameless

2. (   )

  = to just say "hi"

3. (   )

  = to be written all over one's face

4. (   )

  = to blush; to be angry

5. (   )

  = to look great, healthy

Check the answers on **p. 231**

LESSON 2

To go/come to do something

-(으)러 가다/오다

**Track
03**

In this lesson, we are going to look at the structures -(으)러 가다 and -(으)러 오다. These
two structures are used when talking about going somewhere to do something, or coming
from a place in order to do something. -(으)러 is listed in the dictionary as a way to indicate
the purpose of an action, but in actual usage, the nuance of "purpose" is often weakened. If
you want to emphasize the meaning of "in order to", you can use the expression -(으)려고 or
the more formal 위해서 (see Level 3 Lesson 17). When talking about everyday activities, the
two structures -(으)러 가다 and -(으)러 오다 are quite common and are extremely useful to
know.

Examples

놀러 가다 = 놀다 + -(으)러 + 가다

Literal translation: to go "in order to" play

Natural translation: to go "and" hang out; to hang out

고기 잡으러 가다 = 고기 + 잡다 + -(으)러 + 가다

Literal translation: to go "in order to" catch fish

Natural translation: to go fishing

The same types of meanings also apply to -(으)러 오다. However, -(으)러 오다 can only be used when referring to someone coming to a place where you already are, rather than going to a place where neither of you are present.

Also, in many English expressions where nouns are used, verbs replace those nouns in Korean. For example, "to go to bed" is not 침대로 가다, but rather 자러 가다, which literally means "to go in order to sleep".

Sample Sentences

Track 03

석진 씨요? 운동하러 갔어요.

= Seokjin? He went to the gym.

= Seokjin? He went out to exercise.

저는 이제 자러 갈게요.

= I will go to bed now.

옷 찾으러 왔어요.

= I'm here to pick up my clothes.

점심 먹으러 갈래요?

= Do you want to go for lunch?

영화 보러 가고 싶어요.

= I want to go see a movie.

17

잠깐 인사하러 왔어요.

= I just came by to say "hi" quickly.

또 놀러 오세요!

= Please visit us again.

스키 타러 가자!

= Let's go skiing.

수영하러 갈래요?

= Do you want to go swimming?

여기가 제가 피아노 배우러 가는 곳이에요.

= This is the place where I go to learn to play the piano.

**Track
03**

If you want to add a destination, you can add it either before -(으)러 가다/오다 or between
-(으)러 and 가다/오다.

Examples

저는 이제 방에 자러 갈게요. = I will go to my room to sleep now.
저는 이제 자러 방에 갈게요. = I will go to my room to sleep now.

수영장에 수영하러 갈래요? = Do you want to go to the pool to swim?
수영하러 수영장에 갈래요? = Do you want to go to the pool to swim?

Please note that -(으)러 can only be combined with a verb stem. It cannot be used with suffixes such as -았/었/였-, -(으)ㄹ, or -겠-.

Examples

석진 씨요? 운동했으러 갔어요. (X) → 석진 씨요? 운동하러 갔어요. (O)

저는 이제 자겠으러 갈게요. (X) → 저는 이제 자러 갈게요. (O)

점심 먹을러 갈래요? (X) → 점심 먹으러 갈래요? (O)

Track
03

Sample Dialogue

Track 04

윤아: 은희 씨, 내일 뭐 해요? 쇼핑하러 갈래요?

은희: 내일은 어려울 것 같아요. 현우 씨 집에 놀러 가거든요.

윤아: 진짜요? 현우 씨가 집에 초대했어요?

은희: 네. 현우 씨가 집에 놀러 오라고 했어요.

윤아: 우와, 좋겠네요! 잘 다녀오세요.

Yoona: Eunhee, what are you doing tomorrow? Do you want to go shopping?

Eunhee: I don't think I can tomorrow because I'm going to hang out at Hyunwoo's house.

Yoona: Really? Did Hyunwoo invite you over?

Eunhee: Yes. He told me to come hang out at his house.

Yoona: Wow, sounds fun! Have a good time!

✏ Exercises for Lesson 2

Check the answers on **p. 231**

Rewrite the following using -(으)러 가다 *or* -(으)러 오다 *to make the sentence sound more natural or colloquial.*

I. 옷 찾기 위해 왔어요.

→ .... = I'm here to pick up my clothes.

2. 수영하기 위해 갈래요?

→ .... = Do you want to go swimming?

3. 잠깐 인사하기 위해 왔어요.

→ .... = I just came by to say "hi" quickly.

4. 석진 씨요? 운동하기 위해 갔어요.

→ .... = Seokjin? He went to the gym.

5. 여기가 제가 피아노 배우기 위해 가는 곳이에요.

→ .... = This is the place where I go to learn to play the piano.

LESSON 3

I know it is... but it is still

아무리 -(이)라지만, 아무리 -(ㄴ/는)다지만

Track 05

In this lesson, we are going to learn how to use 아무리, which we covered in Level 7 Lesson 14, with the ending -라지만 or -다지만 to talk about something that is too excessive or not considered appropriate. When used together as a set in a sentence, the sentence can take on various meanings depending on the specific context, so pay close attention to the sample sentences.

1. 아무리 -(이)라지만
2. 아무리 -(ㄴ/는)다지만

The above phrases basically have the meaning of, "I know it is so-and-so but it is still too excessive/not appropriate/a bad idea/impossible/incomprehensible."

First, let us take a look at 아무리, which was previously introduced in Level 7 Lesson 14. To briefly recap what we learned in that lesson, 아무리 is often used with -아/어/여도 to mean "no matter how much you do something" or "no matter how something is so-and-so".

22

아무리 비싸도 살 거예요.

= I will buy it no matter how expensive it is.

아무리 바빠도 밥은 먹어야 돼요.

= No matter how busy you are, you have got to eat.

아무리 어려워도 포기하지 않을 거예요.

= No matter how hard it is, I will not give up.

Those are some sample sentences that use 아무리 -아/어/여도. Keeping this usage of 아무리 in mind, let us take a look at today's grammar structures.

(1) 아무리 + NOUN + -(이)라지만

Rule: If the noun ends with a consonant, it is followed by -이라지만. If it ends with a vowel, it is followed by -라지만.

(2) 아무리 + VERB STEM + -ㄴ/는다지만 (action verb)

Rule: If the verb stem ends with a consonant, it is followed by -는다지만. If it ends with a vowel, it is followed by -ㄴ다지만.

(3) 아무리 + VERB STEM + -다지만 (descriptive verb)

Rule: Verb stems of a descriptive verb (예쁘다, 춥다, 빠르다, etc.) are followed by -다지만.

Those are the three variations of today's grammar point. They commonly have one of the following meanings:

    — I know it is so-and-so, but it is still...

    — It is true that it is so-and-so, but it is still...

    — Sure, it is so-and-so, but still...

In essence, you are acknowledging one fact and then presenting another, usually contrasting, viewpoint. 아무리 has the meaning of "no matter how (much)", and -지만 has the meaning of "but", so when combined, they form a sentence pattern that has one of the meanings above.

Sample Sentences

🎙️
Track 05

아무리 친구라지만, 어떻게 그런 부탁을 할 수 있을까?

  = I know she is a friend, but how can she ask me for such a favor?

아무리 가족이라지만, 이해할 수 없어요.

  = I know he is family, but I cannot understand him.

아무리 가까운 친구라지만, 돈을 허락 없이 쓰면 안 돼요.

  = I know you are close friends, but you cannot use his money without his permission.

아무리 요즘 인기가 많다지만, 너무 비싸요.

  = I know it is popular these days, but it is too expensive.

아무리 사람을 많이 만난다지만, 어떻게 다혜 씨를 기억 못 해요?

  = (Talking to Dahye) I know he meets a lot of people, but how does he not remember you?

아무리 잘 먹는다지만, 어떻게 피자 세 판을 먹어요?

  = I know he eats a lot, but how can he eat three pizzas?

아무리 바쁘다지만, 전화는 할 수 있잖아요?

= I know he is very busy, but he can make a phone call, can't he?

아무리 그렇다지만, 이건 너무했네요.

= I know it is true, but this was too much.

Please note that it sounds more natural to use 아무리 -아/어/여도 when talking directly about yourself and the listener to the listener. For example, if you complain to your friend about someone who does not call you, you can say, "아무리 바쁘다지만, 전화는 할 수 있잖아요? (= I know he is very busy, but he can make a phone call, can't he?)" However, if you are talking directly to the person who does not call you, it is more natural to say, "아무리 바빠도 전화는 할 수 있잖아요? (= I know you are very busy, but you can make a phone call, can't you?)"

Track 05

25

Sample Dialogue

Track
06

경화: 희주 씨, 회사 옆에 우동집 있잖아요.
거기 진짜 유명한 데래요. 준배 씨가 어제
점심 먹으러 갔는데 한 시간 기다렸대요.

희주: 네? 한 시간요? 아무리 유명한
집이라지만 그렇게 오래 기다려야
된다고요?

경화: 두 시간 기다렸다는 사람도 있어요. 근데
그 집 우동 진짜 맛있대요.

희주: 아무리 그렇다지만 우동 하나 먹기
위해서 몇 시간을 기다려야 하는 건 좀
심하네요.

Kyung-hwa: Heeju, you know, there's an udon place next to our office. I heard that it's a very famous place. Joonbae said that he went there for lunch yesterday, and he waited for an hour.

Heeju: What? One hour? I know it's a famous place, but you need to wait for that long?

Kyung-hwa: There's also someone who said that they waited for two hours. People say that the udon there is really good, though.

Heeju: However good it may be, having to wait hours for a bowl of udon is a little too much.

✐ Exercises for Lesson **3**

Rewrite the following using 아무리 -(ㄴ/는)다지만 *or* 아무리 -(이)라지만.

1. 아무리 그래도 이건 너무했네요.

  = Even if it is true, this was too much.

→ ....

  = I know it is true, but this was too much.

2. 아무리 가족이어도, 이해할 수 없어요.

  = Even though he is family, I cannot understand him.

→ ....

  = I know he is family, but I cannot understand him.

3. 아무리 가까운 친구여도, 돈을 허락 없이 쓰면 안 돼요.

  = No matter how close of friends you are with him, you cannot use his money without his permission.

→ ....

  = I know you are close friends, but you cannot use his money without his permission.

Check the answers on **P. 231**

🖉 *Exercises for Lesson 3*

4. 아무리 잘 먹어도, 어떻게 피자 세 판을 먹어요?

   = No matter how much he can eat, how can he eat three pizzas?

   → ....

   = I know he can eat a lot, but how can he eat three pizzas?

5. 아무리 바빠도, 전화는 할 수 있잖아요?

   = No matter how busy you are, you can make a phone call, can't you?

   → ....

   = I know he is very busy, but he can make a phone call, can't he?

Check the answers on **p. 231**

LESSON 4

Suggesting Choices

-(이)나, -(이)라도

In this lesson, we are going to learn how to use the grammar point -(이)나 to suggest or choose an option that is perhaps not the most desirable. We will also cover how -(이)나 differs from -(이)라도.

Track
07

-(이)나

> *Conjugation*
>
> Noun ending with a consonant + -이나
> Noun ending with a vowel + -나

In Level 6 Lesson 18, we introduced -(이)나 as a way to say "either A or B". Let us recap briefly.

커피나 우유 = coffee or milk
밥이나 빵 = rice or bread

29

집이나 사무실 = home or office

In these examples, you are not actually choosing between A and B, but rather saying that either A or B will suffice or be applicable. This is the basic usage of -(이)나. Now, we will learn another way to use -(이)나.

When to use -(이)나

You can use -(이)나 to suggest or choose an option that is perhaps not the most desirable or the most interesting at the time. With this usage, the meaning of -(이)나 is similar to "just" in English. If what you really want is a proper 5-course meal, but all you have time for right now is a sandwich, you can say, "I will just have a sandwich (because that is all that is available to me now even though it is not the best option)." Or if your friend has a big test coming up but wants to join you at a party, you can tell them, "Just prepare for your test (and do not think about partying even though partying is what you want)." -(이)나 can be used in these situations.

Sample Sentences

저는 피자나 먹을게요.

= I will just eat pizza.

* *Potential hidden meaning:* I know pizza is not what I want to eat the most, and there are better things to eat if I go out to eat with you, but I will compromise and just eat this pizza because I have something to do now or am feeling lazy.

저는 그냥 청소나 할게요.

= I will just do some cleaning.

* *Potential hidden meaning:* There are other things I would rather do, but I cannot do them right now so I will clean the house, at least for now, until the situation becomes more favorable for me.

저는 집에서 TV나 볼게요.

= I will just watch TV at home.

    * *Potential hidden meaning:* I know watching TV at home is probably not the most productive activity I can do now, but all my plans have been canceled, the weather is not so great, and I am feeling lazy on top of that. So I guess I will just stay at home and watch TV.

숙제나 빨리 해.

= Just hurry up and do your homework.

    * *Potential hidden meaning:* You probably do not want to do your homework now, and there are more exciting things you have in mind, but you should just do what you have to do.

빨리 라면이나 끓여.

= Stop wasting time and just make some ramyeon noodles.

    * *Potential hidden meaning:* You were going to make some ramyeon, but then you were distracted by something more exciting to talk about. Making ramyeon is probably not the most attractive activity for you right now, but just do it.

Track 07

More Sample Sentences

빨리 앉기나 해.

= Just sit down.

빨리 오기나 해.

= Just come over here.

이거나 보고 말해.

= Just look at this before saying anything.

다른 이야기 그만하고 이거나 빨리 결정합시다.
= Let's stop talking about other things, and just decide this one thing.

휴대폰 새로 사려고 생각하지 말고 지금 쓰는 거나 잘 써.
= Do not think about buying a new phone, and just use your current one.

내일 주말인데 영화나 볼까요?
= It is the weekend tomorrow. Shall we watch a movie?

내일은 집에서 그냥 게임이나 할 거예요.
= I will just play video games at home tomorrow.

When to use -(이)라도

In Level 5 Lesson 15, we introduced -(이)라도 as a way to suggest that something is not the best option out of all the available choices. Let us compare this with -(이)나 to see how these two expressions are different.

1. 피자나 먹을게요.
    = I will just eat pizza (even though there are other options).

    피자라도 먹을게요.
    = I would be willing to eat pizza (if there is nothing else available because I am really hungry).
    * In both cases, you are implying that pizza is not the first thing you want to eat. Using 피자나 indicates that you could find other options if you tried, but using 피자라도 implies that pizza is really the only option you have, and you need to be happy with it.

2. 청소나 할게요.

   = I will just clean.

   청소라도 할게요.

   = I will do the cleaning at least.

   * In both cases, you do not necessarily want to clean. Using 청소나 indicates that you could find other things to do if you tried, but using 청소라도 implies that cleaning is not what you want to do most, but you will do it because there is no better option.

3. TV나 볼게요.

   = I will just watch TV.

   TV라도 볼게요.

   = If there is nothing else I want to do, I will at least watch TV or something.

   * TV라도 more strongly implies that watching TV is not a fun activity and is something that you have to resort to because there is nothing else to do.

Track
07

4. 이거나 결정합시다.

   = Let's just decide this.

   이거라도 결정합시다.

   = Let's at least decide this.

   * 이거나 carries the meaning of, "Let's not talk about other things. This is the priority now." On the other hand, 이거라도 has the meaning of, "We cannot decide anything else so let's decide this one thing at least."

33

Sample Dialogue

Track 08

승완: 주연 씨, 이번 주말에 뭐 할 거예요?

주연: 약속 있었는데 취소됐어요. 그래서 집에서 일이나 하려고요.

승완: 하루 종일 집에만 있으려고요?

주연: 저녁에는 나가서 산책이라도 해야죠. 승완 씨는 주말에 약속 있어요?

승완: 저도 약속 없어요. 요즘 날씨 너무 좋으니까 혼자 나가서 자전거라도 타려고요.

Seung-wan: Jooyeon, what are you going to do this weekend?

Jooyeon: I had plans, but they got canceled. So, I'm thinking of just working.

Seung-wan: You're going to stay home all day long?

Jooyeon: I will take a walk in the evening at least, of course. Do you have any plans this weekend, Seung-wan?

Seung-wan: I don't have plans either. The weather is really good these days, so I'm thinking of going out by myself and riding a bike at least.

✏️ Exercises for Lesson 4

Fill in the blanks using either –(이)나 *or* –(이)라도.

1. 이거 (　　　　　) 결정합시다. = Let's at least decide this.

2. 이거 (　　　　　) 결정합시다. = Let's just decide this.

3. 피자 (　　　　　) 먹을게요. = I will just eat pizza (even though there are other options).

4. 피자 (　　　　　) 먹을게요. = I would be willing to eat pizza (if there is nothing else available because I am really hungry).

5. 청소 (　　　　　) 할게요. = I will do the cleaning at least.

6. 청소 (　　　　　) 할게요. = I will just clean.

7. TV (　　　　　) 볼게요. = I will just watch TV.

8. TV (　　　　　) 볼게요. = If there is nothing else I want to do, I will at least watch TV or something.

Check the answers on **p. 231**

35

LESSON 5

To decide to, To agree to

-기로 하다

In this lesson, we will take a look at how to use -기로 하다 to talk about what you have decided or agreed to do. You can talk about plans, decisions, or rules using this sentence ending. It can be used flexibly with various tenses. -기로 했어요 in the past tense can be used to talk about plans or decisions, and -기로 해요 and -기로 하죠 in the present tense can be used to make suggestions.

Conjugation

Verb stem + -기로 하다

If you break down the structure of -기로 하다, you can see that the verb is first turned into the -기 noun form. Then -로 is added, which represents a method or direction. You also use -(으)로 in situations where you are talking about a choice you are making, like in 이걸로 할게요, which means, "I will buy this one." (Here, 이걸로 is short for 이것으로.) Putting everything together, the structure -기로 하다 takes on the meaning of "to decide or choose to do something in this way".

Sample Sentences

어떻게 하기로 했어요?

= What have you decided to do?

> * When talking about plans, 어떻게 (= how) is often used to mean "what" you are going to do, in the sense that you are talking about "how" to deal with the situation.

내일 다시 만나기로 했어요.

= We have decided to meet again tomorrow.

내일 같은 시간에 여기서 만나기로 해요.

= Let's meet again here at the same time tomorrow.

따로 가기로 했어요.

= We have decided to go separately.

Track 09

어디에서 만나기로 했어요?

= Where are you going to meet?

공항에서 바로 만나기로 했어요.

= We have decided to meet directly at the airport.

그건 취소하기로 했어요.

= I have decided to cancel that.

이거 안 하기로 하지 않았어요?

= Haven't we agreed to not do this?

우리 다음에는 계획 먼저 세우기로 해요.

= Next time, let's make plans first.

37

10시에 만나기로 했는데 아직 아무도 안 왔어요.

= We were supposed to meet at 10 o'clock, but nobody is here yet.

There are a few other verbs that can also be used with -기로.

- 약속하다 = to promise

    Ex)

    10시에 만나기로 약속했는데 아직 아무도 안 왔어요.

    = We promised to meet at 10 o'clock, but nobody is here yet.

- 정하다 = to decide

    Ex)

    다 같이 가기로 정했으면 같이 가야죠!

    = If we decided to go all together, we must go together!

- 결정하다 = to decide

    Ex)

    다른 거 사기로 결정했어요?

    = Have you decided to buy a different one?

- 마음먹다 = to make up one's mind

    Ex)

    운동 열심히 하기로 마음먹었어요.

    = I have made up my mind to work out hard.

Sample Dialogue

Track
10

준배: 저 오늘부터 하루에 30분씩 운동하기로 마음먹었어요.

다혜: 그래요? 저 오늘부터 예지 씨랑 같이 운동하기로 했는데, 준배 씨도 같이 할래요?

준배: 아, 정말요? 좋아요. 몇 시에 만나기로 했어요?

다혜: 7시요. 호수 공원으로 오세요. 아! 그리고 운동 빠질 때마다 벌금 천 원씩 내기로 했어요.

*벌금 = fine; penalty

Joonbae: I have made up my mind to exercise for 30 minutes every day starting today.

Dahye: Have you? Yeji and I have decided to exercise together starting today. Do you want to join?

Joonbae: Oh, really? Sounds good. What time are you going to meet?

Dahye: At seven o'clock. Come to Lake Park. Ah! And we have decided to pay 1,000 won as a penalty every time we skip working out.

39

✏ *Exercises for Lesson* **5**

Fill in the blanks using **-기로 하다**. *All the sentences are in* **존댓말**.

1. 이거 ( )?

= Haven't we agreed to not do this?

2. 공항에서 바로 ( ).

= We have decided to meet directly at the airport.

3. 우리 다음에는 ( ).

= Next time, let's make plans first.

4. 내일 같은 시간에 ( ).

= Let's meet again here at the same time tomorrow.

5. ( ) 아직 아무도 안 왔어요.

= We were supposed to meet at 10 o'clock, but nobody is here yet.

LESSON **6**

Advanced Idiomatic Expressions 13

일 (Work)

This is an Advanced Idiomatic Expressions lesson related to 일, which means "work". In order to fully understand and use the expressions introduced in this series, it is essential that you understand the grammatical structure of the sentences. When you come across a grammar point that you are unfamiliar with, please go back and review the related TTMIK lessons.

Track
11

Keyword: **일** = work

1. 일을 쉬다 = to not be working, to be between jobs

쉬다 means "to rest" and in this context, rather than referring to taking a break during working hours, it means that you are not employed at the moment. It usually has the meaning of being "temporarily between jobs", so it cannot be used to describe someone who is in retirement and has no plans to start working again. You can say "일을 쉬고 있어요" when you are either looking for a new job or taking a leave from your current job.

41

Ex)

요즘 일을 잠깐 쉬고 있어요.

= I am not working at the moment.

2. 일할 맛이 나다 = to find it enjoyable to work, to be motivated to work

맛 means "taste", and 맛이 나다 means "to taste like" something. For example, 이상한 맛이 나다 means "to taste strange". 일할 맛, therefore, translates to "the taste to work". What this phrase actually means, however, is that working is enjoyable and fun because of factors like a good working environment, close relationships with your coworkers, high pay, etc.

Ex)

요즘에 주문이 별로 안 들어와서 일할 맛이 안 나요.

= There are not many orders coming in these days, so I do not feel motivated to work.

3. 일 복이 많다 = to have a lot of work coming in

복 means "luck" or "good fortune". To describe someone who has a lot of work coming in, generally or just at the moment, you can say 일 복이 많다, which means "to have a lot of work-related luck". Sometimes you will also hear the phrase 일 복을 타고 나다, which means "to be born with a lot of luck related to work", or "to be destined to never struggle to find work".

Ex)

일 복이 너무 많으셔서 그래요. 일 좀 줄이세요.

= It is because you are a magnet for work. Cut down on some work.

Ex)

요즘 일 복이 터졌어요.

= I am blessed with a lot of work these days.

4. 일을 벌이다 = to start something new, to start a new (potentially unnecessary) project

벌이다 means "to start a project or event", "wage a war", or "stage a protest". The passive voice form of 벌이다 is 벌어지다, which translates to "to happen" or "to take place". 일을 벌이다 means "to start a new project", or "to stir up some new trouble". Depending on the context, it is often used to criticize someone who is starting something new unnecessarily even though they are already busy with other things.

Track
11

Ex)

왜 자꾸 새로운 일을 벌여요? 원래 하던 거부터 마무리해요.

= Why do you keep starting something new? Finish what you were working on first.

5. 일하고 결혼하다 = to know nothing but work, to be always working

결혼하다 means "to get married", and so 일하고 결혼하다 means "to be married to one's work". It refers to someone who is always working and never doing anything else.

Ex)

그 사람은 맨날 일밖에 안 해요. 일하고 결혼했어요.

= He does nothing but work. He is married to his job.

6. 일이 잘 풀리다 = to work out well, to be resolved well

풀다 means "to resolve" or "untie" something, and the passive voice, 풀리다, means "to be resolved". So 일이 잘 풀리다 means that something either went well, or a problem was resolved smoothly.

Ex)
요즘은 일이 잘 풀려서 스트레스를 안 받아요.
= Everything is working out smoothly these days, so I am not stressed.

It is often used in the negative form as well.

Ex)
일이 잘 안 풀리니까 포기하고 싶어요.
= Because things are not working out smoothly, I want to give up.

7. 일이 손에 안 잡히다 = cannot focus on work

잡다 means "to grab" or "hold" something. The passive voice of 잡다 is 잡히다, and means "to be grabbed" or "to be held". It also has the meaning of "can be held". So 일이 손에 안 잡히다 means that while you want to focus on working you cannot, usually because you have something on your mind that is worrying or bothering you.

Ex)
오늘 아침에 핸드폰을 잃어버려서 지금 일이 손에 안 잡혀요.
= I lost my phone this morning, so I cannot focus on work now.

44

8. 일밖에 모르다 = to not be interested in anything else but work

-밖에 is used with a negative sentence to form the meaning of "only", so 일밖에 모르다 means "to know only work" or "to know nothing but work". It is used to describe a person whose only interest is work.

Ex)

그 사람은 일밖에 몰라서 주말에도 맨날 바빠요.

= He is not interested in anything else but work, so he is always busy even on the weekend.

9. 볼일 = something to take care of; an errand to run

Track 11

보다 means "to see", but in the expression 볼일, its meaning is closer to "to tend to" or "to take care of". So 볼일 can be an errand you need to run or something you need to take care of. Two verbs that are commonly used with 볼일 are 보다 and 있다. 볼일을 보다 usually means "to take care of an errand or task", but in a very casual setting, it can also refer to going to the bathroom. 볼일이 있다 means "to have something to take care of".

Ex)

볼일이 있어서 잠깐 해외에 나와 있어요.

= I am overseas for a short while to take care of something.

10. 일도 아니다 = to be very easy to do; to be a piece of cake

Literally translated, this phrase means "to not even be work". It is used to refer to something that is very easy to do.

45

Ex)

저한테 이 정도는 일도 아니죠.

= For me, this is a piece of cake.

11. 일이 산더미처럼 쌓여 있다 = to have a lot of work; to be loaded with work

산 means "mountain" and 더미 means "pile". 쓰레기 더미 is a pile of trash, and 빚더미 is a pile of debt. 산더미 (pronounced 산떠미) is used figuratively to mean "a mountain of" something. It does not refer to an actual mountain.

Ex)

아침 일찍 출근했는데 아직도 일이 산더미처럼 쌓여 있어요.

= I came to work early in the morning, but I still have a ton of work to do.

Track 11

12. 되는 일이 없다 = nothing works out

되다 here means "to be fulfilled well" or "to be accomplished well", so this phrase literally means "nothing is fulfilled well" or "nothing is accomplished well". When things do not work out as you expected or planned, you can use this expression.

Ex)

저는 왜 이렇게 되는 일이 없을까요?

= Why on earth do you think things do not work out for me?

46

Sample Dialogue

Track 12

석준: 화연 씨, 지금 아르바이트 몇 개 하고 있어요?

화연: 두 개요. 근데 다음 주부터 한 개 더 하기로 했어요. 요즘 정말 일 복이 터졌어요.

석준: 너무 일밖에 모르는 거 아니에요? 일하고 결혼한 사람 같아요.

화연: 괜찮아요. 이 정도는 저한테 일도 아니에요.

석준: 그렇다면 다행이지만... 그래도 쉬엄쉬엄하세요.

* 쉬엄쉬엄하다 = *to take it easy, to take it slow*

Sukjun: Hwa-yeon, how many part-time jobs are you working now?

Hwa-yeon: Two, but I've decided to take on one more starting next week. I am a magnet for work these days.

Sukjun: Aren't you too invested in your work? You're like a person who is married to their work.

Hwa-yeon: I'm fine. This doesn't even feel like work to me.

Sukjun: That's a relief if so... but you should still take it easy sometimes.

Check the answers on **p. 231**

✏️ Exercises for Lesson **6**

Fill in the blanks with the appropriate idioms with 일 *from the lesson.*

1. ( )

    = nothing works out

2. ( )

    = something to take care of; an errand to run

3. ( )

    = to have a lot of work; to be loaded with work

4. ( )

    = cannot focus on work

5. ( )

    = to work out well, to be resolved well

LESSON 7

Listing Possible Scenarios

-거나, -(ㄴ/는)다거나

Track 13

In Level 6 Lesson 18, we learned that there are multiple expressions for saying "or" in Korean, including -(이)나, -거나, and 아니면. Depending on the type of words you are linking, different words are used to express "or". When linking verbs, you use -거나. Let us review with some example sentences.

Ex)

비가 오면 집에서 영화를 보거나 책을 읽어요.

= When it rains, I watch a movie or read a book at home.

이걸로 음악을 듣거나 영화를 볼 수 있어요.

= You can listen to music or watch movies with this.

그 사람은 지금 회사에 있거나 체육관에 있을 거예요.

= I think he is either at his office or at the gym now.

* Because you are making an assumption here, -을 거예요 is used even though the sentence is in the present tense.

49

However, you might have heard some people say "verb stem ＋ -(ㄴ/는)다거나" instead of "verb stem ＋ -거나".

Ex)

이걸로 음악을 듣는다거나 영화를 볼 수 있어요.

= You can listen to music or watch movies with this.

-(ㄴ/는)다거나 is a combination of -(ㄴ/는)다 and -거나, but when listing two or more facts, -거나 and -(ㄴ/는)다거나 are interchangeable.

Track 13

Ex)

비가 오면 집에서 영화를 보거나 책을 읽어요.

= 비가 오면 집에서 영화를 본다거나 책을 읽어요.

= When it rains, I watch a movie or read a book at home.

이걸로 음악을 듣거나 영화를 볼 수 있어요.

= 이걸로 음악을 듣는다거나 영화를 볼 수 있어요.

= You can listen to music or watch movies with this.

Sometimes, people attach -거나 or -(ㄴ/는)다거나 to both verb stems, and add an extra verb, 하다. This structure implies that there are more possible scenarios beyond the examples given.

Ex)

비가 오면 집에서 영화를 보거나 책을 읽어요.

= When it rains, I watch a movie or read a book at home.

비가 오면 집에서 영화를 보거나 책을 읽거나 해요.

= When it rains, I do things like watch a movie or read a book at home.

이걸로 음악을 듣는다거나 영화를 볼 수 있어요.

= You can listen to music or watch movies with this.

이걸로 음악을 듣는다거나 영화를 본다거나 할 수 있어요.

= You can do things like listen to music or watch movies with this.

As a note, the set -(ㄴ/는)다거나 -(ㄴ/는)다거나 하다 is used much more commonly than -거나 -거나 하다.

Sample Sentences

저는 일요일에는 영화를 본다거나 책을 읽는다거나 해요.

= On Sundays, I do things like watch a movie or read a book.

옷이 안 맞는다거나 마음에 안 든다거나 하면 가서 다른 걸로 바꾸세요.

= If the clothes do not fit, or if you do not like them, go change into something else.

Track 13

조금 춥다거나 열이 난다거나 하면 바로 알려 주세요.

= If you are a little cold or have a fever or something, please let me know right away.

저는 노래를 부른다거나 그림을 그린다거나 하면서 스트레스를 풀어요.

= I relieve stress when I do things like sing or draw.

When are -거나 and -(ㄴ/는)다거나 NOT interchangeable?

Since using -(ㄴ/는)다거나 puts more emphasis on the "listing examples" aspect, you cannot replace -거나 with -(ㄴ/는)다거나 when you use -거나 to mean "either A or B".

51

그 사람은 지금 회사에 있거나 체육관에 있을 거예요. (natural)

= I think he is either at his office or at the gym now.

* 그 사람은 지금 회사에 있다거나 체육관에 있을 거예요. (unnatural)

In addition, when you list just some of all the examples possible, it is more natural to use -(ㄴ/는)다거나 than -거나.

Ex)

A: 아이들 키우면서 어떨 때 제일 힘들어요?

= What is the hardest part about raising children?

B: 그럴 때 제일 힘들죠. 아프다거나, 둘이 싸운다거나... (more natural)

= You know, the hardest times are when they are sick or when they fight and stuff.

B: 그럴 때 제일 힘들죠. 아프거나, 둘이 싸우거나... (less natural)

* If you say "아프거나, 둘이 싸우거나...", it sounds more like you are saying, "Either when they are sick or when they fight."

Sample Conversations

I. A: 저는 스킨십 별로 안 좋아해요.

= I don't really like physical contact with people.

B: 스킨십요?

= Physical contact?

A: 네. 손을 잡는다거나, 팔짱을 낀다거나, 그런 거요.

= Yeah, like holding hands or linking arms, things like that.

2. A: 경화 씨는 왜 회사 그만뒀대요?

  = Did you hear about the reason why Kyung-hwa quit her job?

     B: 특별한 이유는 없대요.

     = She said that there was no special reason.

  A: 에이, 설마요. 이유가 있었겠죠. 회사에 너무 싫어하는 상사가 있었다거나, 다른 회사에서 더 좋은 조건으로 오라고 했다거나.

  = No way. There must have been a reason, like a boss she really hated, or maybe another company made her a better offer.

3. A: 혼자 밥 먹을 때도 이렇게 예쁜 그릇에 먹어요?

  = Do you eat your food off pretty plates like this even when you eat alone?

     B: 아니요. 집에 손님이 온다거나, 음식 사진을 찍는다거나, 그럴 때만 예쁜 그릇을 꺼내죠.

     = No. I only take out the pretty plates for times like when a guest comes over, or when I take photos of the food.

Track 13

Sample Dialogue

주연: 현우 씨는 기분이 안 좋다거나
스트레스를 받는다거나 할 때 어떻게
해요?

현우: 저는 그럴 때 공부를 한다거나 일을
해요.

주연: 네? 기분이 안 좋은데 공부를 한다고요?

현우: 농담이에요. 왜요? 지금 기분 안
좋아요?

*Jooyeon: Hyunwoo, what do you do when you feel
down or stressed out?*

Hyunwoo: When that happens, I study or work.

*Jooyeon: What? You're saying that you study when
you don't feel good?*

*Hyunwoo: I'm kidding. Why? You're not feeling
good right now?*

🖉 Exercises for Lesson **7**

1. Which of the following most strongly implies that there are more possible scenarios other than watching movies or reading books?

① 비가 오면 집에서 영화를 보거나 책을 읽어요.

② 비가 오면 집에서 영화를 보거나 책을 읽거나 해요.

③ 비가 오면 집에서 영화를 본다거나 책을 읽어요.

2. Which sentence is NOT natural?

① 그 사람은 지금 회사에 있거나 체육관에 있을 거예요.

② 그 사람은 지금 회사에 있다거나 체육관에 있을 거예요.

3. Select the sentence that can mean, "You can either listen to music or watch movies with this."

① 이걸로 음악을 듣거나 영화를 볼 수 있어요.

② 이걸로 음악을 듣는다거나 영화를 볼 수 있어요.

③ 이걸로 음악을 듣는다거나 영화를 본다거나 할 수 있어요.

Check the answers on **p. 231**

✏ *Exercises for Lesson* **7**

Write the phrase that can fill in the two blanks.

4.

조금 춥 .... 열이 난 .... 하면 바로 알려 주세요.

= If you are a little cold or have a fever or something, please let me know right away.

Answer: ( )

5.

A: 아이들 키우면서 어떨 때 제일 힘들어요?

= What is the hardest part about raising children?

B: 그럴 때 제일 힘들죠. 아프 .... , 둘이 싸운 .... ···

= You know, the hardest times are when they are sick or when they fight and stuff.

Answer: ( )

LESSON **8**

While Keeping the Current State

-(으)ㄴ/는 채로

Listing two actions using "while"

Track
15

When you talk about doing one action "while" doing another action, you can use the basic grammar point -(으)면서. It can be used in sentences like the following.

Ex)

집에 가면서 음악을 들었어요.

= I listened to music while I was going home.

일을 하면서 커피를 마셨어요.

= I drank coffee while I was working.

As shown in the examples above, -(으)면서 is used when talking about two actions that are happening at the same time. However, there is a different grammar point you must use when listing two states or one action and one state.

Linking one state with another state or action using "while"

The main word to understand in this grammar point is 채. 채 is a "dependent noun" (의존명사 in Korean), which means that it can only be used as part of a longer expression.

채 means "the way it is right now" or "the existing state", and is usually followed by -로. 채로 can be used in the following forms depending on whether the main verb is conjugated into the past tense or the present tense.

An action that happened in the past: -(으)ㄴ 채로
An action that is taking place right now: -는 채로

Note that the "tense" we are referring to above is not the tense of the entire sentence. The entire sentence itself can be in any tense. Let us take 앉다 as an example.

앉다 means "to sit". 앉은 is the past tense modifier form for 앉다. "Someone who sat" is 앉은 사람, and "the place where I sat" is 제가 앉은 곳. So if you use 앉은 채로, it means that you have sat down, and you are maintaining that state.

Ex)
앉은 채로 = while seated; still sitting
앉은 채로 잤어요. = I slept while seated.
앉은 채로 자고 있어요. = He/She is sleeping while seated.
앉은 채로 잘거예요. = I will sleep while seated.

Sample Sentences
앉은 채로 들으세요.
= Listen to me while remaining seated.

앉은 채로 두 팔을 높이 들어 보세요.

= Try raising both of your arms high while seated.

앉은 채로 옆으로 조금만 가 보세요.

= Try moving slightly to the side while seated.

If you look at the sentences above, the action of "sitting down" has already happened in the (near) past. You are already seated, and it is your current state. You are linking this current state with another action.

More examples

Track
15

옷을 입다 = to put on clothes
옷을 입은 채로 수영장에 들어갔어요. = I went into the swimming pool while still wearing my clothes.

신발을 신다 = to put on shoes
신발을 신은 채로 방에 들어갔어요. = I went into the room while still wearing my shoes.

컵을 손에 들다 = to hold a cup in one's hand
컵을 손에 든 채로 뛰었어요. = I ran while holding the cup in my hand.

침대에 눕다 = to lie down on the bed
침대에 누운 채로 영화를 봤어요. = I watched a movie while lying on my bed.

안경을 쓰다 = to put on glasses
안경을 쓴 채로 선크림을 발랐어요. = I put on some sunblock while wearing my glasses.

59

Dropping -로 at the end

While -(으)ㄴ 채로 is the full expression, the particle -로 is also commonly dropped.

컵을 손에 든 채로 뛰었어요.

= I ran while holding the cup in my hand.

= 컵을 손에 든 채 뛰었어요.

안경을 쓴 채로 선크림을 발랐어요.

= I put on some sunblock while wearing my glasses.

= 안경을 쓴 채 선크림을 발랐어요.

Track
15

When is -는 채로 used?

-는 채로 is used with verbs like 있다, 없다, 알다, and 모르다 that describe a state rather than an action.

Sample Sentences

교과서를 잃어버려서 책이 없는 채로 학교에 갔어요.

= I lost my textbooks, so I went to school without them.

저는 아무것도 모르는 채로 그 방에 들어갔어요.

= I went into that room without knowing anything.

In colloquial Korean, people often say 모른 채로 instead of 모르는 채로. It is technically grammatically incorrect, but its usage like this is usually accepted.

저는 아무것도 모르는 채로 그 방에 들어갔어요.

= 저는 아무것도 모른 채로 그 방에 들어갔어요.

-는 채로 can still be used with action verbs when you want to emphasize something that is ongoing. However, when used like this the verb is usually used in the present progressive tense.

Sample Sentences

아이를 울고 있는 채로 놔두고 왔어요.

= I left a crying baby.

컵을 손에 들고 있는 채로 뛰었어요.

= I ran while holding the cup in my hand.

Track 15

61

Sample Dialogue

Track
16

예지: 사무실에서 앉은 채로 할 수 있는 운동이
　　　있을까요?

동근: 그럼요. 제가 하나 알려 드릴게요. 먼저,
　　　두 다리를 앞으로 쭉 뻗으세요.

예지: 그리고요?

동근: 두 다리를 쭉 뻗은 채로 발목을 앞뒤로
　　　움직이세요. 어때요? 시원하죠?

예지: 오, 정말 시원하네요. 고마워요!

*Yeji: Do you think there are some exercises that
you can do while seated in the office?*

*Dong-geun: Sure. Let me show you one. First,
stretch your legs out in front of you.*

Yeji: And then?

*Dong-geun: With your legs stretched straight out,
move your ankles back and forth. How is it?
Doesn't it feel nice?*

Yeji: Oh, it's really nice! Thanks!

✏ Exercises for Lesson **8**

Fill in the blanks using **-(으)ㄴ/는 채로**.

1. (   ) 두 팔을 높이 들어 보세요.

    = Try raising both of your arms high while seated.

2. 신발을 (   ) 방에 들어갔어요.

    = I went into the room while still wearing my shoes.

3. 컵을 손에 (   ) 뛰었어요.

    = I ran while holding the cup in my hand.

4. 저는 아무것도 (   ) 그 방에 들어갔어요.

    = I went into that room without knowing anything.

5. 옷을 (   ) 수영장에 들어갔어요.

    = I went into the swimming pool while still wearing my clothes.

Check the answers on **p. 232**

LESSON **9**

Verb Endings -(으)ㄴ/는걸(요) and -(으)ㄹ걸(요)

-(으)ㄴ/는걸(요), -(으)ㄹ걸(요)

Track
17

In this lesson, we are going to look at a sentence ending that you can hear particularly often in Korean song lyrics. It is 걸(요), and the syllable 걸 is often used as word play for the English word "girl" because of its similar sound.

걸(요) is not actually used by itself, but rather in the form of either -(으)ㄴ/는걸(요) or -(으)ㄹ걸(요). These two sentence endings are very interesting and can express quite specific meanings. They can also usually be replaced with something else, although when doing so their nuanced meaning can be slightly lost. In this lesson, we will introduce some of these alternative sentences as well.

There are four different ways these endings are used. The ending -(으)ㄴ/는걸(요) is used (1) to show exclamation when you find out something new, and (2) when giving supporting evidence or facts while explaining or claiming something. The ending -(으)ㄹ걸(요) is used (3) when making an assumption about something, and (4) when expressing regret about something you did or did not do in the past.

64

Let us take a look at the four different usages in more detail. Except for sentences that use the fourth usage, expressing regret about something you did or did not do in the past, you can end your sentence with either a period or a question mark. Ending your sentence with a question mark gives the impression that you are expecting a reply from your listener.

Usage 1

When you discover something new and find it interesting or amazing, you can use -(으)ㄴ/는걸(요). This usage is much less common in real life than usage (3).

Track
17

Sample Sentences

이거 생각보다 어려운걸요.

= I find this to be more difficult than I thought.

= 이거 생각보다 어려운데요.

의외로 재미있는걸요?

= Surprisingly, I find that it is fun!

= 의외로 재미있네요.

오! 실제로 보니 더 좋은걸?

= Oh, this looks better in person!

= 오! 실제로 보니 더 좋은데?

Usage 2

When giving supporting evidence or facts while explaining something or making a claim, you

65

can use -(으)ㄴ/는걸(요). This usage is also less common than usage (3).

Sample Sentences

그런데 항상 제가 제일 일찍 도착하는걸요.

= But I am always the first to arrive!

= 그런데 항상 제가 제일 일찍 도착해요.

저는 그 사람 이름도 모르는걸요.

= I don't even know that person's name!

= 저는 그 사람 이름도 몰라요.

어제 벌써 이메일을 보냈는걸요.

= I already sent the email yesterday!

= 어제 벌써 이메일 보냈어요.

Track 17

Usage 3

When making an assumption about something, you can use -(으)ㄹ걸요. This is the most common usage of -걸(요). Because of -(으)ㄹ, the ending looks like it is in the future tense, but -(으)ㄹ걸요 is used to show your assumption about the past, the present, or the future. Please note that -(으)ㄹ걸요 is only used in response to what someone else has said.

Sample Sentences

아마 오늘 그 가게 문 안 열걸요.

= That store will probably not be open today.

= 아마 오늘 그 가게 문 안 열 것 같아요.

경은 씨도 이미 알걸요.

= I think Kyeong-eun already knows.

= **경은 씨도 이미 알 거예요.**

마케팅 회의요? 오늘 세 시일걸요.

= The marketing meeting? It is probably at 3 o'clock today.

= **마케팅 회의요? 오늘 세 시일 거예요.**

주연 씨한테 말해 보세요. 자기가 하겠다고 할걸요?

= Try asking Jooyeon. I assume she will say she wants to do it herself.

= **주연 씨한테 말해 보세요. 자기가 하겠다고 할 거예요.**

공연 벌써 시작했을걸요?

= I am sure the show has already started.

= **공연 벌써 시작했을 것 같아요.**

Track
17

Usage 4

When expressing regret about something you should or should not have done, you can also use -(으)ㄹ걸. Please note that even though -(으)ㄹ is usually used for the future tense, this usage of -(으)ㄹ conveys regret about the past. In this instance, you do not end the sentence in -요 because you are talking to yourself. Also, unlike usages (1), (2), and (3), rather than raising the tone of your voice at the end of the sentence, you lower the tone of your voice.

Sample Sentences

내가 그냥 참을걸.

= I should have just held back.

= **내가 참지 않은 게 후회돼.**

회사 들어오기 전에 여행 좀 많이 다닐걸.

= Before I joined the company, I should have traveled more.

= **회사 들어오기 전에 여행 많이 안 다닌 게 후회돼.**

어제 공부 좀 더 하고 잘걸.

= I should have studied a little more before I went to bed yesterday.

= **어제 공부 더 안 하고 잔 게 후회돼.**

If you would like to say that you should NOT have done something, you can use -지 말걸, which is a combination of -지 말다 and -(으)ㄹ걸.

파마하지 말걸.

= I should not have gotten my hair permed.

머리 자르지 말걸.

= I should not have had my hair cut.

If you would like to express regret directly to another person, rather than talking to yourself, you can use the form -(으)ㄹ걸 그랬어요, as in 어제 공부 좀 더 하고 잘걸 그랬어요.

Sample Dialogue

Track 18

준배: 예지 씨 사무실에 있겠죠?

경은: 퇴근했을걸요.

준배: 아, 예지 씨한테 할 말 있었는데...
　　　아까 나오기 전에 얘기할걸.

경은: 오늘 꼭 해야 하는 말이면 문자
　　　보내세요. 아마 바로 확인할걸요.

Joonbae: Yeji should be in the office, right?

Kyeong-eun: I think she left.

Joonbae: Ah! I had something to say to her. I should
　　　have talked to her earlier today before I
　　　left the office.

Kyeong-eun: If it's something you need to tell her
　　　today, text her. She'll probably check your
　　　message right away.

🖊 Exercises for Lesson 9

Choose the sentence that has the same meaning as the underlined part of the dialogue.

Check the answers on **p. 232**

1.

A: 경화 씨, 저 사람이랑 친해요?

B: 네? 저는 저 사람 이름도 모르는걸요.

① 저는 저 사람 이름도 모르는 게 후회돼요.

② 저는 저 사람 이름도 모르는 바보예요.

③ 저는 저 사람 이름도 몰라요.

2.

A: 지나 씨, 머리 잘랐어요?

B: 네. 아, 근데 머리 자르지 말걸.

① 머리 자른 게 후회돼요.

② 머리 자르지 마세요.

③ 머리 자르지 않았는데요.

3.

A: 소희 씨, 내일 가게 쉰다고 경은 씨한테 말해 주세요.

B: 경은 씨도 이미 알걸요.

① 경은 씨도 이미 알고 있는 걸 후회하고 있어요.

② 경은 씨도 이미 알 거예요.

③ 경은 씨도 이미 알아요.

✏ Exercises for Lesson **9**

4.

A: 다혜 씨는 사무실 비밀번호 몰라도 돼요. 제일 일찍 도착하는 사람만 알면 돼요.

B: 항상 제가 제일 일찍 도착하는걸요.

① 항상 제가 제일 일찍 도착하는 게 후회돼요.

② 항상 제가 제일 일찍 도착할 거예요.

③ 항상 제가 제일 일찍 도착해요.

5.

A: 승완 씨, 이 퀴즈 풀어 보세요.

B: 이거 생각보다 어려운걸요.

① 이거 생각보다 어려워서 후회돼요.

② 이거 생각보다 어려울 거예요.

③ 이거 생각보다 어려운데요.

Check the answers on **p. 232**

71

LESSON 10

Sentence Building Drill 18

Sentence Building Drill 18

Track
19

In this series, we focus on how to use the grammatical rules and expressions that you have previously learned to train yourself to comfortably make Korean sentences.

We will start off with THREE key sentences and practice changing different parts of these sentences so that you do not end up simply memorizing the same three sentences. We want you to be able to make Korean sentences as flexibly as possible.

Key Sentence (1)

원래 오늘 친구랑 만나기로 했는데, 일이 산더미처럼 쌓여 있어서 못 나갔어요.

= I was originally supposed to meet up with my friend, but I could not go out because I had a ton of work piled up.

Key Sentence (2)

요즘 아무리 일이 바쁘다지만, 잠깐은 만날 수 있잖아요.

= I know you are really busy these days, but we can meet for just a little bit, can't we?

Key Sentence (3)

저는 헬스장에 간다거나 공원에 산책하러 간다거나 할 때는 항상 음악을 듣는 편이에요.

= I always tend to listen to music when I go to the gym or go for a walk in the park.

Expansion & Variation Practice with Key Sentence (1)

0. Original Sentence:

원래 오늘 친구랑 만나기로 했는데, 일이 산더미처럼 쌓여 있어서 못 나갔어요.

= I was originally supposed to meet up with my friend, but I could not go out because I had a ton of work piled up.

1.

Track 19

원래 오늘 친구랑 만나기로 했는데 = I was originally supposed to meet up with my friend

원래 오늘 친구 집에 가기로 했는데 = I was originally supposed to go to my friend's place

원래 어제 전화를 주기로 했는데 = They were originally supposed to call me yesterday

원래 내일까지 끝내기로 했는데 = I was originally supposed to finish it by tomorrow

원래 지난 토요일까지 받기로 했는데 = I was originally supposed to receive it by last Saturday

2.

일이 산더미처럼 쌓여 있어서 못 나갔어요.

= I could not go out because I had a ton of work piled up.

일이 아직도 산더미처럼 쌓여 있어요.

= I still have a ton of work piled up.

일이 아직도 산더미 같아요.

= I still have a ton of work.

퇴근해야 되는데 일이 산더미처럼 쌓여 있어요.

= I have to get off work, but I have a ton of work piled up.

73

일이 산더미처럼 쌓여 있는데 어디 갔어요?

= We have a ton of work piled up. Where did you go?

Expansion & Variation Practice with Key Sentence (2)

0. Original Sentence:

요즘 아무리 일이 바쁘다지만, 잠깐은 만날 수 있잖아요.

= I know you are really busy these days, but we can meet for just a little bit, can't we?

1.

요즘 아무리 일이 바쁘다지만

= I know you are really busy these days, but

요즘 아무리 시간이 없다지만

= I know you really do not have time these days, but

요즘 아무리 우리가 만날 시간이 없었다지만

= I know we really have not had time to meet lately, but

요즘 아무리 이게 유행이라지만

= I know this is really in fashion these days, but

요즘 아무리 제가 텔레비전을 많이 본다지만

= I know I watch a lot of television these days, but

Track 19

2.

잠깐은 만날 수 있잖아요. = We can meet for just a little bit, can't we?

잠깐은 통화할 수 있잖아요. = We can talk on the phone for just a little bit, can't we?

잠깐은 이야기할 수 있잖아요. = We can talk for just a little bit, can't we?

잠깐은 앉았다 갈 수 있잖아요. = You can take a seat for just a little bit, can't you?

잠깐은 들어올 수 있잖아요. = You can come in for just a short while, can't you?

Expansion & Variation Practice with Key Sentence (3)

0. Original Sentence:

저는 헬스장에 간다거나 공원에 산책하러 간다거나 할 때는 항상 음악을 듣는 편이에요.

= I always tend to listen to music when I go to the gym or go for a walk in the park.

1.

저는 헬스장에 간다거나 공원에 산책하러 간다거나 할 때는

= when I go to the gym or go for a walk in the park

친구들을 만난다거나 모임에 간다거나 할 때는

= when I meet my friends or go to a gathering

요리를 한다거나 청소를 한다거나 할 때는

= when I cook or clean the house

공부를 한다거나 책을 읽는다거나 할 때는

= when I study or read a book

영화를 본다거나 게임을 한다거나 할 때는

= when I watch a movie or play games

Track
19

2.

항상 음악을 듣는 편이에요. = I always tend to listen to music.

항상 이 옷을 입는 편이에요. = I always tend to wear these clothes.

항상 이 카페에 가는 편이에요. = I always tend to go to this cafe.

항상 산책을 하는 편이에요. = I always tend to go for a walk.

항상 집에만 있는 편이에요. = I always tend to just stay home.

Sample Dialogue

은희: 보람 씨, 오늘 희주 씨 만나죠?

보람: 아, 원래 만나기로 했는데, 희주 씨가 일이
산더미처럼 쌓여 있다고 취소했어요.

은희: 정말요? 아무리 일이 많다지만, 어떻게
약속을 당일에 취소해요?

보람: 하하. 저희 둘은 원래 당일에도 약속을
여러 번 바꾸는 편이에요.

* 당일 = on the day of the event, on the due date

Eunhee: Boram, you're seeing Heeju today, right?

Boram: Ah, we were originally supposed to meet,
but Heeju said that she has a ton of work
piled up and canceled.

Eunhee: Really? I know she has a lot of work to
do, but how can she cancel plans on the
day of?

Boram: Haha. We both have the tendency to
change our plans several times even on
the day of.

✏ Exercises for Lesson 10

Check the answers on **p. 232**

Fill in the blanks to match the English translation.

1. (   ) 음악을 듣는 (   )이에요.

   = I always tend to listen to music.

2. 요즘 (   ) 이게 유행이라지만

   = I know this is really in fashion these days, but

3. (   ) 오늘 친구랑 만나(   ) 했는데

   = I was originally supposed to meet up with my friend

4. 친구들을 만난다거나 모임에 (   )

   = when I meet my friends or go to a gathering

5. 퇴근해야 되는데 일이 (   )처럼 쌓여 있어요.

   = I have to get off work, but I have a ton of work piled up.

Seaweed
(김)

If you know anything about Korea, you will have certainly heard of seaweed, the amazing food that is known as gim (김) in Korean. There are a variety of ways to eat this dish, and all of them are amazing. But do you know the history of gim? When did Koreans start eating it? How was it eaten in the past? Let us take a trip into the past and learn a bit about this dish that we all enjoy so much. Afterwards, we will explore a few of the ways you can prepare gim and bring a bit of Korea into your home.

Some of the earliest mentions of seaweed being eaten in Korea date back to the Silla dynasty, a Korean kingdom that existed from 57 BC to 935 AD. Some books say that during the Silla dynasty seaweed was used as part of a family's dowry. However, the seaweed used then is thought to have been harvested from rocks, rather than being farmed like it is today.

There are a few legends floating around about how seaweed was first discovered. Some of the more popular stories revolve around a person finding a log covered in seaweed floating in the water. According to one story, seeing the seaweed on the log gave people the idea to grow the plant on bamboo poles, which makes sense seeing how it was originally cultivated using bamboo or oak poles. Over time, Koreans eventually began using nets instead of poles to grow seaweed. Even rafts are said to have been used to grow large quantities of seaweed.

Today, it is estimated that 19,000 tonnes of seaweed is grown every year. To grow this much seaweed, Koreans still use rafts and racks. Racks are used to grow seaweed by planting bamboo poles into the seabed and attaching nets between them. Seeds are then added to the nets. Once the seeds are attached to the nets, they are moved to a farming area until they are ready to be harvested.

Now that we have gone over a bit of history about when Koreans began using seaweed and how it is grown, let us get into the tasty side of it and talk about how you can enjoy this fantastic dish.

I am sure you have heard about the first way to eat seaweed, which is using it to wrap rice. This dish is called gimbap. I would venture to say that the majority of people have heard of this dish. It is a fairly simple dish to make, as long as you have some cooked rice and sheets of seaweed to wrap the rice in. This is a great meal to take with you on a picnic or when hiking. And since there are so many different ingredients you can use to prepare this meal, you will be able to find one that suits your tastes. The most basic gimbap recipe uses sliced vegetables, rice, seaweed, and ham. After it is rolled, the gimbap

is usually salted, and olive oil is added with a few sesame seeds sprinkled on top. It gets its name from the Korean words gim (김), which means seaweed, and bap (밥), which means rice. So next time you are trying to think of what to prepare for a picnic, try your hand at making some gimbap rolls. If you want to keep it super simple, you can just roll up some rice in some seaweed and it will be just as tasty.

During my time in Korea, another way I have become accustomed to eating seaweed is eating it like a chip. This might sound strange to some of you, but it is quite normal over here. In fact, some places actually serve seaweed with a small dish of soy sauce as a kind of appetizer.

If you have a hankering for something salty but want to try to stay on the healthy side, why not try eating some dried seaweed? If you have big sheets of seaweed in your house, you can chop them into tiny squares and prepare a small dish of soy sauce. While binge-watching your favorite Korean drama, enjoy this snack that is a bit better for you than a normal bag of potato chips.

Another dish that you may or may not have heard of is a seaweed cookie. This is for those who like snacks that are both sweet and salty. Like a lot of Korean dishes, these delicious snacks come in a variety of shapes. One type you can find is round sticks with seaweed cooked into the cookie. There are also versions that are round and flat with seaweed sprinkled in the center.

However, one of my favorite ways to eat seaweed is simply to crush it up and add it to some rice and minced vegetables. After mixing it up, grab a handful of the rice and shape it into a ball. This riceball is called "jumeok-bap (주먹밥)", which literally means "fist rice". It is super easy to make and is a great snack for both kids and adults. In fact, this is a fun dish you can make together with kids. These also make a great meal for a picnic or to pack into your kid's lunch box when they go to school.

Since seaweed has become so popular all over the world, more and more people are creating new ways of using seaweed in their dishes. In fact, I think I have made myself hungry and am craving some seaweed now. I guess it is time for me to make a seaweed snack for myself.

Written by Johnny Bland

우와!

벌써 Lesson 10까지 공부했네요!

다음 레슨에는 어떤 재미있는 표현이 기다리고 있을까요?

LESSON 11

Expressing Assumptions

-(으)ㄹ 텐데

Track 21

In this lesson, you will learn how to use -(으)ㄹ 텐데 to express an assumption about a certain situation. When using this grammar point, your assumption is always accompanied by a suggestion, doubt, or question.

The construction of -(으)ㄹ 텐데

-(으)ㄹ 텐데 is the shortened form of -(으)ㄹ 터인데.

The key element here is 터, which originally means a "place" or a "spot". It is not commonly used on its own, but you can find it in many compound words and idiomatic expressions.

놀이터 = playground for kids

쉼터 = rest area

공터 = vacant lot

전쟁터 = battlefield

낚시터 = fishing spot

터를 잡다 = to pick out a location

터를 닦다 = to establish the foundation

Translated literally, -(으)ㄹ 터 means "a place to do" something or "a place where something will happen". The actual meaning of 터 in real-life sentences is "situation". So you can think of -(으)ㄹ 터 as a "situation", "context", or "circumstance" in which something will happen.

So all together, -(으)ㄹ 텐데 has the meaning of, "looking at the situation, I can see that A will happen or is happening" or, "judging from the circumstances, it must be like this".

Sample Sentences

바쁠 텐데 나중에 이야기해요. (suggestion)

= You must be busy. Let's talk later.

Track 21

피곤할 텐데 앉아서 좀 쉬어요. (suggestion)

= You must be tired. Take a seat and get some rest.

제 전화번호 알 텐데 왜 전화를 안 했을까요? (question)

= I'm sure he knows my number. I wonder why he did not call me.

밖에 추울 텐데 괜찮을까요? (doubt)

= It must be cold outside. Will it be okay?

Omitting the following clause

When a sentence ends with -(으)ㄹ 텐데 and is not followed by another statement, you can

85

assume that a suggestion, doubt, or question exists but has been omitted.

이거 비쌀 텐데...

= This must be expensive.

= 이거 비쌀 텐데 (왜 샀어요?)

아닐 텐데...

= That cannot be true.

= 아닐 텐데 (왜 그렇게 말하는 거예요?)

피자 곧 올 텐데.

= The pizza will be delivered soon.

= 피자 곧 올 텐데 (어디 가요?)

Track 21

Do not use -(으)ㄹ 텐데 for a fact that everybody knows

-(으)ㄹ 텐데 can only be used to express an assumption. If you do not know the time and are just guessing, you can say, "벌써 세 시 거의 다 됐을 텐데요 (= It must be close to 3 o'clock)." However, if you can actually see the clock on the wall, using -(으)ㄹ 텐데 in a sentence sounds unnatural.

-(으)면 -(으)ㄹ 텐데

-(으)ㄹ 텐데 is often used with -(으)면 to express the speaker's hopes or wishes.

Sample Sentences

너도 같이 가면 좋을 텐데.

= It would be nice if you were also coming with us.

친구랑 같이 살면 재밌을 텐데.

= It would be fun if I lived together with my friend.

조금 덜 더우면 좋을 텐데.

= It would be nice if it was a bit less hot.

-았/었/였으면 -았/었/였을 텐데

You can use the past tense suffix -았/었/였- with -(으)면 -(으)ㄹ 텐데 to express that you wish a situation that is contrary to reality would happen, or to wish that something in the past had happened differently.

Track 21

Sample Sentences

여름이었으면 야외 수영장에서 수영했을 텐데.

= If it had been summer, we would have swum in the outdoor swimming pool.

거기에 그 사람이 올 줄 알았으면 나도 갔을 텐데.

= If I had known that he would be there, I also would have gone.

공부 열심히 했으면 시험 더 잘 봤을 텐데.

= If I had studied hard, I would have done better on the exam.

Sample Dialogue

경화: 오늘 월요일이어서 바쁠 텐데 어떻게
왔어요?

두루: 오늘 쉬는 날이에요. 아, 그리고 오늘
경화 씨 생일이죠? 제가 작은 선물을
준비했어요.

경화: 선물요? 우와! 고마워요. 근데 이거...
비쌀 텐데...

두루: 아니에요. 별로 안 비싸요. 근데 주연
씨는 안 왔어요?

경화: 아직 안 왔어요. 오늘 모임 있는 거 알고
있을 텐데, 아직 안 보이네요.

*Kyung-hwa: It's Monday today, and you must be
busy. How did you manage to come here?*

*Duru: It's my day off today. Oh, and Kyung-hwa,
it's your birthday today, right? I've prepared
a small gift for you.*

*Kyung-hwa: A gift? Wow! Thank you. But this must
be expensive.*

*Duru: No, it's not that expensive. By the way, is
Jooyeon not here?*

*Kyung-hwa: She's not here yet. I'm sure she knows
about today's gathering, but I don't see her
here yet.*

88

The Final Step in Talk To Me In Korean's

✏ Exercises for Lesson 11

Fill in the blanks using -(으)ㄹ 텐데.

1. 이거 (   )...

   = This must be expensive.

2. 너도 같이 가면 (   ).

   = It would be nice if you were also coming with us.

3. (   ) 나중에 이야기해요.

   = You must be busy. Let's talk later.

4. 친구랑 같이 살면 (   ).

   = It would be fun if I lived together with my friend.

5. 여름이었으면 야외 수영장에서 (   ).

   = If it had been summer, we would have swum in the outdoor swimming pool.

Check the answers on **p. 232**

LESSON 12

Sharing What You Have Seen or Heard

Track
23

-던데요, -다던데요

In this lesson, we will take a look at the endings -던데요 and -다던데요 as well as some of their variations. These two grammar structures are used to talk about something you experienced, observed, or heard about. You can still convey the same kind of meaning without using these endings, too, but they add more flavor and detail to your sentences.

Although -던데요 and -다던데요 look similar, they are used in very different circumstances. Typically, -던데요 is used to talk about past experiences or observations, and -다던데요 is used to relay information that you heard.

How to use -던데요

-던데요 can be used to talk about something you experienced or witnessed in the past. When using this sentence ending, the speaker is expecting the listener to show a reaction to what they have been told.

90

Conjugation

If the action happened as you were witnessing it

- Verb stem + -던데요

- Noun + -(이)던데요

If the action had already happened when you saw it

- Verb stem + -았/었/였- + -던데요

- Noun + -이었- or -였- + -던데요

Sample Sentences

(The sentences in parentheses are examples of possible interpretations. Other interpretations are possible as well, and depend on the context of the conversation.)

Track 23

어제 갑자기 눈이 오던데요.

= It suddenly snowed yesterday. (I saw it myself! What do you say about that?)

어제 전화 안 하던데요.

= They did not call me yesterday. (You said they would. What happened?)

or

= They did not call me yesterday. (That is how it went. What do you think?)

봤는데, 너무 비싸던데요.

= I saw it, but it was too expensive.

그 사람 한국어 잘하던데요.

= He spoke Korean well! (Didn't you say he does not speak Korean?)

or

= He spoke Korean well! (Did you know that?)

91

오늘 잘하시던데요.

= I saw you doing a good job today.

손님이 오셨던데요.

= It seems like you have a guest. (Are you aware of it?)

그 게임 어제 처음 해 봤는데 생각보다 어렵던데요.

= I tried that game for the first time yesterday, and it was more difficult than I had thought.

그 책 현우 씨한테 이미 빌려줬던데요.

= He/she had already lent the book to Hyunwoo (when I checked).

Note that in all of the sample sentences above, because you are expecting some kind of reaction from the listener, it usually sounds unnatural to just end your conversation there.

How to use -다던데요

You can use -다던데요 to relay to someone a fact or a piece of information that you heard from someone else. -다던데요 is short for -다고 하던데요. In this structure, -다고 하다 means to "say that..." and is combined with the ending -던데요 that was introduced above.

Conjugation

If the action had not happened when you heard about it or the state was true when you heard about it

- Descriptive verb stem + -다던데요
- Action verb stem ending with a vowel or the consonant ㄹ (in this case, ㄹ is dropped) + -ㄴ다던데요

The Final Step in Talk To Me In Korean's

- Action verb stem ending with a consonant (except for the consonant ㄹ) +
-는다던데요
- Noun + -(이)라던데요

If the action had already happened by the time you heard about it or the state was true at one time, but it was not true by the time you heard about it
- Descriptive/Action verb stem + -았/었/였- + -다던데요
- Noun + -이었- or -였- + -다던데요

Sample Sentences

(The sentences in parenthesis are examples and are not the only possible interpretations.)

내일 회의 안 한다던데요.

= I heard that there is no meeting tomorrow. (Were you told otherwise?)

Track 23

수요일에 다시 온다던데요.

= They said they would come back on Wednesday. (What do you think?)

지금은 안 판다던데요.

= I heard they do not sell it now. (What should I do now?)

여행 혼자 간다던데요.

= He told me he is going on the trip alone. (Did you think he was going with someone else?)

거기보다는 여기가 더 넓다던데요.

= I heard it is more spacious here than there. (Shall we choose this place then?)

아직 학생이라던데요.

= I heard she is still a student. (That is not what YOU heard, right?)

이렇게 하면 된다던데요.

= They said that you can just do it like this.

다혜 씨도 점심 사무실에서 먹는다던데요.

= I heard that Dahye also eats her lunch in the office.

미국에 있을 때는 선생님이었다던데요.

= I heard that he/she was a teacher when he/she was in the United States.

준배 씨가 청소했다던데요.

= I heard that Joonbae cleaned it up.

Track 23

Sample Dialogue

Track 24

화연: 혹시 석준 씨 한국 돌아왔어요?

윤아: 아니요. 다음 달에
　　　돌아온다던데요.

화연: 그래요? 어제 사무실 앞을
　　　지나가던데...

윤아: 잘못 봤겠죠. 아직
　　　캐나다라던데요.

Hwa-yeon: By any chance, is Sukjun back in Korea?

*Yoona: No. I heard that he's coming back next
month.*

*Hwa-yeon: Is that so? I thought I saw him pass by
our office yesterday.*

*Yoona: You must have been mistaken. I heard he's
still in Canada.*

✏ *Exercises for Lesson 12*

Choose the option that best fits in the blank.

1.

경화: 너무 떨려서 잘 못할 것 같다고 하시더니, _____?

지나: 그래요? 감사합니다.

① 오늘 잘하셨어요

② 오늘 잘하시던데요

2.

예림: 밖에 손님이 오셨어요.

승완: 아, 그래요? 대표님! 밖에 _____.

① 손님이 오셨대요

② 손님이 오셨던데요

Check the answers on **p. 232**

3.

경은: 왜 그 방법으로 하고 있어요?

윤아: 석진 씨가 _____? 왜요? 이렇게 하는 거 아니에요?

① 이렇게 하면 된대요

② 이렇게 하면 된다던데요

4.

소희: 예지 씨, 그 게임 해 봤어요?

예지: 네. 어제 처음 해 봤는데, ...

① 생각보다 어려웠대요

② 생각보다 어렵던데요

5.

보람: 거기랑 여기 중에서 어디가 더 넓을까요?

다혜: 준배 씨가 .... :

① 거기보다는 여기가 더 넓던데요

② 거기보다는 여기가 더 넓다던데요

Check the answers on **p. 232**

LESSON 13

As a result of

-는 바람에

Track
25

There are several ways to indicate a reason for something. The expression that is most commonly used is 때문에. You can also use the phrase 덕분에 to mean "thanks to". While 때문에 can be either neutral or negative, 덕분에 is usually positive.

The grammar point for this lesson, **-는 바람에**, is generally used to talk about a negative result or an outcome that was not the most ideal. 바람 means "wind", so you can think of -는 바람에 as "in the wind of" something that happened.

> **Structure**
> Verb stem (reason) **+ -는 바람에 +** outcome (in the past tense)

Ex)

실수를 하는 바람에 = as a result of making a mistake

넘어지는 바람에 = as a result of falling over

갑자기 친구가 들어오는 바람에 = as a result of my friend suddenly coming in

제 친구가 사람들한테 다 말하는 바람에 = as a result of my friend telling everyone

98

휴대폰을 떨어뜨리는 바람에 = as a result of dropping my cellphone

Replacing -는 바람에 with -아/어/여서

In most contexts, -는 바람에 can be replaced with -아/어/여서, but when doing so the emphasis on a "negative outcome" is lost because -아/어/여서 is more neutral. For example, the phrase 제 친구가 사람들한테 다 말하는 바람에 sounds like it will be followed by a negative result, whereas 제 친구가 사람들한테 다 말해서 can be followed by either a negative or a positive result.

- Negative result with -는 바람에

  Ex)
  제 친구가 사람들한테 다 말하는 바람에, 우리 비밀 계획을 모두 알게 됐어요.
  = As a result of my friend telling everyone, they all found out about our secret plan.

Track 25

- Neutral result with -아/어/여서

  Ex)
  제 친구가 사람들한테 다 말해서, 모두 도와서 일을 빨리 끝냈어요.
  = My friend told everyone, so everybody helped and we finished the work early.

  Sample Sentences
  컴퓨터가 갑자기 고장 나는 바람에 숙제가 다 지워졌어요.
  = My computer suddenly broke down, so my homework got deleted.

  지갑을 집에 놓고 오는 바람에 선물을 못 샀어요.
  = I left my wallet at home, so I could not buy a present.

99

오늘 아침에 늦게 일어나는 바람에 수업에 지각했어요.

= I got up late this morning, so I was late for class.

Idiomatic expressions using 바람

The word 바람 itself, which means "wind", also has many interesting idiomatic usages. Now let us look at some of the most commonly used idiomatic expressions related to 바람.

1. 무슨 바람이 불어서

= why; why suddenly

* *literal translation:* what kind of wind blew in order for

Track 25

Ex)

무슨 바람이 불어서 이렇게 일찍 일어났어요?

= Why did you get up so early, unlike how you usually get up?

2. 바람을 넣다

= to inflate, to tempt someone to do something (undesirable)

* *literal translation:* to put in air

Ex)

자전거 타이어에 바람 좀 넣어야 돼요.

= I need to put some air in my bike tires.

Ex)

공부 열심히 하고 있는 애한테 왜 바람을 넣어요?

= The kid is studying hard now. Why tempt him (to do something that's not as desirable as studying)?

3. 바람맞다

= to be stood up

* *literal translation:* to be hit with wind, to have wind blown at oneself

Ex)

친구랑 약속 있어서 나갔는데 바람맞았어요.

= I had plans to meet with a friend, but I was stood up.

4. 바람을 쐬다

= to get some fresh air

Ex)

집중이 안 돼서 바람 좀 쐬고 올게요.

= I cannot focus, so I will go out and get some fresh air.

Track 25

5. 잠옷 바람으로

= while still in one's pajamas

* This is used when you leave the house in your pajamas, without having the time to change into other clothes.

Ex)

전화 받고 급하게 나오느라 잠옷 바람으로 나왔어요.

= I came out in a hurry after getting a phone call, so I came out in my pajamas.

Sample Dialogue

Track
26

예지: 준배 씨, 늦어서 미안해요. 버스를 잘못 타는 바람에...

준배: 아, 그랬군요. 전화했는데 안 받아서 걱정했어요.

예지: 핸드폰을 집에 두고 오는 바람에 연락할 방법이 없었어요. 많이 기다렸죠?

준배: 아니에요. 괜찮아요.

Yeji: Joonbae, I'm sorry I'm late. I got on the wrong bus, so...

Joonbae: Oh, I see. I was worried since you didn't answer my call.

Yeji: I left my phone at home, so there was no way to contact you. Have you been waiting long?

Joonbae: No, I haven't. It's okay.

✏ Exercises for Lesson 13

Fill in the blanks by choosing the phrase that best completes the sentence.

Check the answers on **p. 232**

1.

> • 모두 도와서 일을 빨리 끝냈어요
> • 우리 비밀 계획을 모두 알게 됐어요

(1) 제 친구가 사람들한테 다 말해서, ...

(2) 제 친구가 사람들한테 다 말하는 바람에, ...

2.

> • 숙제가 다 지워졌어요
> • 새 컴퓨터를 샀어요

(1) 컴퓨터가 갑자기 고장 나서 ....

(2) 컴퓨터가 갑자기 고장 나는 바람에 ....

3.

> • 선물을 못 샀어요
> • 다혜 씨한테 얻어먹었어요

(1) 지갑을 집에 놓고 와서 ....

(2) 지갑을 집에 놓고 오는 바람에 ....

    * 얻어먹다 = *to be treated to food*

103

✏ Exercises for Lesson 13

4.

> - 깜짝 놀랐지만 반가웠어요
> - 다 들켰어요

(1) 갑자기 친구가 들어와서 ....

(2) 갑자기 친구가 들어오는 바람에 ....

5.

> - 수업에 지각했어요
> - 안 피곤해요

(1) 오늘 아침에 늦게 일어나서 ....

(2) 오늘 아침에 늦게 일어나는 바람에 ....

Check the answers on **p. 232**

LESSON **14**

Expressing Reactions

-다니/라니

When you see or hear something that is very interesting, ridiculous, or hard to believe, you can express your reaction by using the grammar structure -다니/라니. This structure is used in various forms based on what comes before it.

Track
27

> ### *Conjugation*
>
> Present tense:
>
> Verb stem + -다니
>
> Noun + -(이)다 or -이/가 아니다 + -라니
>
> Past tense:
>
> Verb stem + -았/었/였다니
>
> Noun + -(이)다 or -이/가 아니다 + -었/였다니

When using this structure, you first mention the "circumstance", followed by -다니/라니, and then express your reaction to the circumstance. Your reaction is usually expressed through phrases like 신기하다 (to be interesting), 믿을 수가 없다 (to be impossible to believe), 화가

105

나다 (to be upsetting), 말이 안 되다 (to make no sense), and more.

Sample Sentences

5월에 눈이 오다니 너무 신기하네요.

= It is so interesting that it is snowing in May.

또 거짓말을 하다니 정말 화가 나네요.

= It makes me so angry that they lied again.

이게 백만 원이라니 너무 비싼 거 아니에요?

= This costs 1,000,000 won? Isn't it too expensive?

아직도 안 왔다니 이게 말이 되나요?

= He is still not here? Can you believe it?

저 사람이 범인이 아니라니 말도 안 돼.

= He is not the culprit? No way.

Omitting the part after -다니/라니

When it is easy to guess the speaker's intended meaning after -다니/라니, the phrase following -다니/라니 is often omitted. In these instances, the sentence ends with -다니! or -라니! as an exclamation. The exact translation of these kinds of sentences depends on the context of the conversation.

5월에 눈이 오다니!

= (I cannot believe that) it is snowing in May!

The Final Step in Talk To Me In Korean's

또 거짓말을 하다니!

= (I cannot believe that) he lied again!

이게 100만 원이라니!

= This costs 1,000,000 won! (It is ridiculous!)

-(ㄴ/는)다니

-(ㄴ/는)다니, which is short for -(ㄴ/는)다고 하니, has another usage. As you learned in Level 5 Lesson 17, -(ㄴ/는)다고 하다 means "to say that S + V", and -니 is the same as -니까. Therefore, -(ㄴ/는)다니 literally means "since someone says that S + V".

Track 27

Ex)
제이슨 씨도 한국어를 공부하신다니 제 책을 드릴게요.
= Since you said that you are also studying Korean, Jason, let me give you my book.

은희 씨 이사 간 집은 회사에서 가깝다니 다행이네요.
= I heard that Eunhee's new house is close to the office. That's a relief.

-(ㄴ/는)다니 can also be used to express your reaction when you see or hear something that is very interesting, ridiculous, or hard to believe.

Ex)
제이슨 씨가 한국을 떠난다니!
= (I cannot believe that) Jason is leaving Korea!

이걸 익히지도 않고 먹는다니!
= (I cannot believe that) you eat this uncooked!

107

Then, what is the difference between -다니 and -(ㄴ/는)다니?

Using -다니 implies that you are expressing your reaction as you experience something, whereas using -(ㄴ/는)다니 implies that you are expressing your reaction to something after hearing about it.

Ex)

(1)

제이슨 씨가 한국을 떠나다니!

= (I cannot believe that) Jason is leaving Korea! / (I cannot believe that) Jason has left Korea!

제이슨 씨가 한국을 떠난다니!

= (I heard and I cannot believe that) Jason is leaving Korea!

You can say the first sentence either as you hear the news that Jason is leaving Korea, or right after you find out that Jason has just left Korea. However, you cannot say the second sentence if Jason has already left Korea. If he has already left, you would say 제이슨 씨가 한국을 떠났다니!

(2)

이걸 익히지도 않고 먹다니!

= (I cannot believe that) you are eating this uncooked! / (I cannot believe that) you just ate this uncooked!

이걸 익히지도 않고 먹는다니!

= (I heard and I cannot believe that) you eat this uncooked!

You can say the first sentence either as you watch someone eating something uncooked or right after you see someone eating something uncooked. You cannot say the second sentence if someone has already eaten something uncooked.

Since -(ㄴ/는)다고 can be used to quote future tense sentences, you can also express your reaction with -(ㄴ/는)다니 when you see or hear something about the future. You cannot talk about the future with -다니.

Ex)
제이슨 씨가 다음 달에 한국을 떠나다니! (unnatural)
제이슨 씨가 다음 달에 한국을 떠난다니! (natural)
= (I cannot believe that) Jason is leaving Korea next month!

-(으)라니

Track 27

When someone tells you to do something and you find it very interesting, ridiculous, or hard to believe, you can express your reaction using -(으)라니, which is short for -(으)라고 하다니.

Sample Sentences

이걸 혼자 다 하라니 말도 안 돼요.
= Telling me to do this all by myself makes no sense.

두 시간 걸려서 왔는데 다시 집에 가라니! 싫어요.
= Are you telling me to go back home, even though it took me two hours to come here? I don't want to.

팔 굽혀 펴기를 100개 하라니... 하고 싶어도 못 해요.
= (I cannot believe that) you are telling me to do 100 push-ups. I cannot do it even if I wanted to.

이렇게 더운데 에어컨을 켜지 말라니 너무해요.
= Telling us not to turn on the air conditioner when it is this hot is so mean.

109

Sample Dialogue

석준: 오늘 수업 휴강이래요.

다혜: 네? 과제 다 했는데 휴강이라니!

석준: 아, 걱정하지 말아요. 과제는 온라인으로 제출하래요.

다혜: 뭐라고요? 휴강인데 과제를 제출하라니 너무하네요.

석준: 과제 다 했다면서요?

* 휴강 = cancellation of a class

Sukjun: They say that today's class is canceled.

Dahye: What? I completed my assignment, and the class is canceled! Unbelievable.

Sukjun: Oh, no worries. They told us to submit it online.

Dahye: What did you say? Telling us to submit the assignment even though the class is canceled is so mean.

Sukjun: But you said you finished your assignment.

✏ Exercises for Lesson 14

1. What would you say when you look at an item that costs 1,000,000 won and think it is ridiculous?

① 이게 100만원이라니!

② 이게 100만원이었다니!

2. What would you say when looking at someone eating something uncooked, which you find unbelievable?

① 이걸 익히지도 않고 먹다니!

② 이걸 익히지도 않고 먹는다니!

3. What would you say when you have just heard that Jason is leaving Korea next month, and you cannot believe it?

① 제이슨 씨가 다음달에 한국을 떠나다니!

② 제이슨 씨가 다음달에 한국을 떠난다니!

③ 제이슨 씨가 다음달에 한국을 떠났다니!

4. What would you say when someone told you to do something all by yourself, which you think makes no sense?

① 이걸 혼자 다 한다니 말도 안 돼요.

② 이걸 혼자 다 하라니 말도 안 돼요.

5. What would you say to someone who you think is mean because they told you not to turn on the air conditioner even though it is really hot?

① 이렇게 더운데 에어컨을 켜지 않으라니 너무해요.

② 이렇게 더운데 에어컨을 켜지 말라니 너무해요.

Check the answers on **P. 233**

111

LESSON **15**

Question Ending -니?

-니?

Track 29

In this lesson, we are going to learn how to use -니 at the end of a 반말 sentence. Although we looked at -다니/라니 in the previous lesson, this sentence ending is unrelated to that grammar structure.

When can you use -니?

You can only use the -니 ending as a question to a child or someone who you are very close to, or when you are talking to yourself and wondering about something out loud. You cannot use it with anyone older than you.

What kind of meaning does it have?

When -니 is added at the end of a sentence, the sentence's general meaning does not change, but the tone of the sentence becomes different. When using -니 at the end of a

112

question, you sound more like an older person talking to a child. You can also use it to scold someone younger than you.

Comparison #1

Regular question: 다들 어디 있어? = Where are you guys?

-니 question: 다들 어디 있니? = Where are you guys? (You are probably an adult talking to a group of children.)

Comparison #2

Regular question: 뭐 해? = What are you doing?

-니 question: 뭐 하니? = What are you doing? (You sound like a teacher or adult talking to a child, or like you are talking to a very close friend who does not mind you talking "down" to them.)

Track 29

Comparison #3 (A mom talking to her child)

Regular question: 엄마가 몇 번 말했어? = How many times did I tell you?

-니 question: 엄마가 몇 번 말했니? = How many times did I tell you? (You sound more upset.)

Usage examples

1. An adult talking to a child (or someone much younger)

꼬마야, 넌 이름이 뭐니?

= Little kid, what is your name?

민송이는 무슨 색깔 좋아하니?

= Minsong, what color do you like?

113

엄마 어디 계시니?

= Where is your mom?

* On rare occasions, you will hear an adult ending a question to other younger adults with -니. This is definitely not polite and shows the speaker's perception of the listener as someone younger or lower that they do not need to show respect toward.

2. Talking to a close friend

When talking to a close friend, some people use -냐 instead of -니. -냐 sounds stronger and is more commonly used by men, while -니 is more commonly used by women. You need to be careful when using this sentence ending, because if the other person does not feel close to you, they might be offended.

Track 29

너는 왜 우니?

= Why are YOU crying?

여기서 혼자 뭐 하니?

= What are you doing alone here?

왜 자꾸 이랬다 저랬다 하니?

= Why do you keep going back and forth about your decision?

3. Poetic usage (especially song lyrics)

여우야, 여우야. 뭐 하니? (a line from a popular children's song)

= Fox, fox. What are you doing?

나의 반쪽을 채워 줄 너는 어디 있는 거니?

= The one who will fill my other half, where are you?

4. Scolding a child or a close friend

너 왜 선생님 말 안 듣니?

= Why do you not listen to your teacher?

너 제정신이니?

= Are you even in your right mind?

너 또 거짓말이니?

= Are you lying again?

5. Talking to oneself

나 뭐 하니?

= What am I even doing?

나 뭐라고 하는 거니?

= What am I talking about?

= What did I just say? (It was ridiculous.)

* You can also use this to respond to what someone else has said by dropping 나 and saying "뭐라고 하는 거니?"

나 오늘 왜 이렇게 예쁘니?

= (Looking in the mirror) Why am I so pretty today?

나 왜 이렇게 멍청하니?

= Why am I so stupid?

115

Sample Dialogue

Track 30

은희: 너 청소 언제 했니? 방이 이게 뭐야.

희주: 왜? 이 정도면 깨끗한 거 아니니?

은희: 뭐라고 하는 거니? 먼지가 이렇게 많이 쌓여 있는데.

희주: 아이참, 너 가면 청소할 거야.

Eunhee: When did you last clean the room? Look at this mess!

Heeju: Why? Isn't this clean?

Eunhee: What are you talking about? Look how much dust has piled up.

Heeju: Give me a break. I am going to clean it after you leave.

✎ Exercises for Lesson 15

Rewrite the following sentences using -니?

1. 꼬마야, 넌 이름이 뭐야?

→ ....

2. 너는 왜 울어?

→ ....

3. 여기서 혼자 뭐 해?

→ ....

4. 너 제정신이야?

→ ....

5. 나 왜 이렇게 멍청해?

→ ....

Check the answers on **p. 233**

117

LESSON **16**

Various Usages of the Ending -게

-게

Track 31

This lesson is about the different ways to use the ending -게. The ending -게 can be used to (1) convert a descriptive verb or adjective into an adverb, or (2) indicate the purpose or aim of an action. We will first take a look at both usages, and then explore the second one more in depth.

Making adverbs

To make an adjective, take the verb stem of a descriptive verb and add -ㄴ or -은.

> **Ex)**
> 작다 (to be small) [verb] → 작은 (small) [adjective]
> 빠르다 (to be fast) [verb] → 빠른 (fast) [adjective]

To make an adverb, instead of -ㄴ or -은, add -게 to the verb stem.

Ex)

작다 (to be small) [verb] → 작게 (in a small amount/on a small scale) [adverb]

빠르다 (to be quick) [verb] → 빠르게 (quickly, at a fast speed) [adverb]

Let us look at some more examples of adverbs ending with -게.

Ex)

이상하다 (to be strange) → 이상하게 = strangely

맛있다 (to be tasty) → 맛있게 = in a tasty way

느리다 (to be slow) → 느리게 = slowly

싸다 (to be cheap) → 싸게 = cheaply, inexpensively, at a cheap price

부드럽다 (to be soft) → 부드럽게 = softly, in a soft manner

The usage of -게 as an adverb ending is easy to understand and can be seen commonly in Korean sentences. However, not every word that ends with -게 is the adverb form of a descriptive verb. There is also another way that -게 can be used.

Track
31

Indicating the purpose or aim of an action

When you see -게 attached to the end of an action verb, it is not being used as an adverb, but rather as an adverbial phrase. In these instances, -게 shows the purpose, aim, or end goal of an action and is often translated to "so that (one can)..." or "in order to".

The difference between an adverb and an adverbial phrase is that adverbs can be used on their own in diverse contexts, whereas adverbial phrases are made specifically for the sentence they are used in.

For example, the verb for "to be slow" is 느리다, and the adverb form of the verb is 느리게.

119

The word 느리게 can be used on its own in diverse contexts. However, let us take a look at the action verb 잡다, which means to catch or to hold. Changing 잡다 to 잡게 does not make it into a pre-existing adverb. Rather, 잡게 can only be used in the specific sentence it was created for. Out of context, 잡게 does not make sense. Please note this difference when using -게 with action verbs.

Basic form

Simply put -게 after a verb stem, and then add a following clause about what needs to be done for the purpose to be achieved.

Sample Sentences

수업을 시작하게 여기로 모이세요.

= Gather here so that we can start the class.

저녁 같이 먹게 빨리 오세요.

= Come here quickly so that we can have dinner together.

일찍 도착하게 서둘러 주세요.

= Please hurry up so that we can arrive early.

People sometimes say what needs to be done first before adding the -게 phrase after to talk about the purpose.

Ex)
여기로 모이세요, 수업을 시작하게.
빨리 오세요, 저녁 같이 먹게.
서둘러 주세요, 일찍 도착하게.

Negative form + -게

You can use 안, 못, or -지 않게 to mean "so that you do not" or "in order not to".

Sample Sentences

비 안 맞게 조심하세요.

= Be careful not to get rained on.

애들이 못 만지게 높은 데에 두세요.

= Put it in a high place so that kids cannot touch it.

넘어지지 않게 조심하세요.

= Be careful not to fall down.

Track
31

-(으)ㄹ 수 있게

Since -게 has the meaning of "so that..." or "in order to", it is often used in conjunction with -을 수 있다 to make the structure -(으)ㄹ 수 있게.

Sample Sentences

마감 기한을 지킬 수 있게 미리 준비해 주세요.

= Prepare in advance so that you can meet the deadline.

멀리서도 볼 수 있게 크게 써 주세요.

= Write it in big letters so that you can see it even from far away.

모두 다 들을 수 있게 큰 소리로 말해 주세요.

= Say it out loud so that everybody can hear you.

121

Alternative expressions

There are two other ways you can express "in order to": -도록 and -기 위해서.

In most of the sentences introduced in this lesson, -게 can be replaced with -도록. Using -도록 instead of -게 makes the sentence sound more formal.

Ex)

모두 다 들을 수 있게

= 모두 다 들을 수 있도록

= So that everybody can hear you

-기 위해서, however, is a very formal expression and cannot replace -게 in many of the sentences used in this lesson. You can only use -기 위해서 when the subject of the first clause and the second clause is the same.

Ex)

모두 다 들을 수 있기 위해서 큰 소리로 말해 주세요. (X)

모두 다 들을 수 있도록 큰 소리로 말해 주세요. (O)

Sample Dialogue

Track
32

경은: 두루 씨, 내일 캠핑 간다고 했죠? 이
　　　모기약 가져가세요, 모기 물리지 않게.

두루: 고마워요. 근데 여름이니까 반바지만
　　　가져가도 되겠죠?

경은: 여름이어도 밤 되면 추울 거예요. 감기
　　　걸리지 않게 긴 옷도 가져가세요.

두루: 아, 그럴 수도 있겠네요. 고마워요.

*Kyeong-eun: Duru, you said you are going camping
tomorrow, right? Take this mosquito
repellent so that you don't get bit by
mosquitoes.*

*Duru: Thanks. Hey, since it's summer, it will be
okay if I just take shorts, right?*

*Kyeong-eun: Even though it's summer, it will get
cold at night. Take pants and long sleeves so
that you don't catch a cold.*

Duru: Ah, maybe you're right. Thanks.

123

✎ Exercises for Lesson 16

Rewrite the following sentences by replacing **-도록** *with* **-게**.

1. 비 안 맞도록 조심하세요.

→ ....

2. 멀리서도 볼 수 있도록 크게 써 주세요.

→ ....

3. 모두 다 들을 수 있도록 큰 소리로 말해 주세요.

→ ....

4. 넘어지지 않도록 조심하세요.

→ ....

5. 마감 기한을 지킬 수 있도록 미리 준비해 주세요.

→ ....

Check the answers on **P. 233**

LESSON 17

It is more of a... than

-(ㄴ/는)다기보다, -(이)라기보다

This lesson is about an expression you can use to rephrase or correct what someone else says, or to make your description about something more accurate. It can be translated to "rather than", "it is more correct to say", or "it is more of a... than...".

Track 33

Conjugation

Present tense:

Action verb stem + -ㄴ/는다기보다

Descriptive verb stem + -다기보다

Noun + -(이)라기보다

Past tense:

Verb stem + -았/었/였다기보다

Noun + -이었다기보다 or -였다기보다

125

Understanding the meaning in more detail

-다기보다 is the shortened form of -다고 하기보다, and -라기보다 is shortened from -라고 하기보다. Both have the meaning of "rather than saying…"

• -보다 is used to compare things and means "than" or "compared to".

• -기 is used to turn a verb into its noun form.

So when using -다 (verb ending) + 기보다 or -라기보다, you are saying "rather than saying A, I think B is a more accurate way to put it". To emphasize the contrast between two descriptions, -는 is commonly added as well to form -다기보다는 or -라기보다는. The overall meaning of the sentence still stays the same with -는 added.

Track
33

Sample Sentences

하기 싫다기보다는, 시간이 안 될 것 같아요.

= It is not really that I do not want to do it, but that I do not think I will have time.

어렵다기보다 시간이 오래 걸려요.

= Rather than being difficult, (it is more accurate to say that) it is time-consuming.

그건 일이라기보다는 취미예요.

= Rather than being work, it is (more of) a hobby.

많이 먹는다기보다는 자주 먹어요.

= It is not really that I eat a lot, but rather that I eat often.

Commonly used structures

There are some words and phrases that are often used in conjunction with -다기보다/라기보다 to make the meaning of the sentence more clear. Some of the examples below use -는 at the end of -다기보다/라기보다, and others do not.

I. 꼭 + -다기보다/라기보다

꼭 means "must, specifically, without fail", and in this structure, it adds the meaning of "not necessarily".

> **Ex)**
> 꼭 제 말이 맞는다기보다, 이런 부분도 생각하자는 거예요.
> = I am not necessarily saying I am right. I am suggesting we should think about this aspect, too.

Track 33

2. -다기보다/라기보다 + -에 가까워요

> **Ex)**
> 이건 일이라기보다는 취미에 가까워요.
> = Rather than being work, it is closer to a hobby.

3. 딱히 + -다기보다/라기보다

When combined with a negative sentence or meaning, 딱히 means "not particularly" or "not specifically".

> **Ex)**
> 딱히 하기 싫다기보다, 안 해도 될 것 같다는 말이에요.

127

= I am not specifically saying that I do not want to do it, but that I feel like I do not have to do it.

4. -다기보다/라기보다 + 그냥

Ex)

저는 스키를 잘 탄다기보다 그냥 좋아해요.

= I am not really good at skiing. It is more accurate to say I just like it.

5. -다기보다/라기보다 + -것 같아요

Ex)

그 사람은 엄청 미남이라기보다는, 특별한 매력이 있는 것 같아요.

= Rather than being incredibly handsome, I think he has his own special charm.

Track 33

6. -다기보다/라기보다 + -(으)ㄴ/는 편이에요

Ex)

그 사람은 머리가 좋다기보다는 노력을 많이 하는 편이에요.

= Rather than being smart, I think he tends to work very hard.

7. -다기보다/라기보다 + -는 거죠

Ex)

하고 싶어서 한다기보다는, 해야 되니까 하는 거죠.

= I do not necessarily do it because I want to, but because I have to.

Sample Dialogue

Track
34

경은: 주연아, 나 너무 많이 먹지 않니?

주연: 언니는 많이 먹는다기보다 먹는 걸
즐기는 거죠.

경은: 그런가? 아, 나 운동도 좀 해야 되는데...

주연: 언니 날씬한데요?

경은: 살을 빼고 싶다기보다 건강을 위해서
운동을 해야 될 것 같아.

*Kyeong-eun: Jooyeon, don't you think I eat too
much?*

*Jooyeon: It's not really that you eat a lot, you just
enjoy eating.*

Kyeong-eun: Is it? Ah, I need to exercise as well.

Jooyeon: But you're slim!

*Kyeong-eun: It's not really that I want to lose
weight, but I think I should exercise for my
health.*

129

✏ *Exercises for Lesson 17*

Fill in the blanks by combining the appropriate Korean word with -(ㄴ/는)다기보다는 *or* -(이)라기보다는*.*

1. 그건 (   ), 취미예요.

    = Rather than being work, it is (more of) a hobby.

2. 많이 (   ) 자주 먹어요.

    = It is not really that I eat a lot, but rather that I eat often.

3. (   ) 시간이 오래 걸려요.

    = Rather than being difficult, (it is more accurate to say that) it is time-consuming.

4. 하기 (   ), 시간이 안 될 것 같아요.

    = It is not really that I do not want to do it, but that I do not think I will have time.

5. 저는 스키를 잘 (   ) 그냥 좋아해요.

    = I am not really good at skiing. It is more accurate to say I just like it.

LESSON 18

Let alone

-은/는커녕

In this lesson, we are going to look at how to use -은/는커녕 to talk about something that is "not even" done or "far from" happening. -은/는커녕 is often translated to "let alone" and is used in sentences with negative meanings. The phrase following -은/는커녕 is usually a worse situation or outcome than whatever comes before -은/는커녕.

Track 35

> ### Conjugation
> Noun + -은/는커녕
> Verb stem + -기 + -는커녕

Ex)

숙제는커녕 = let alone homework

도와주기는커녕 = let alone helping

무섭기는커녕 = let alone being scary, far from being scary but rather...

칭찬은커녕 = let alone a compliment

Commonly used expressions

There are several expressions that are used together with -은/는커녕 to emphasize and complete its meaning. Take a look at some of these common combinations below.

- A는커녕 B도 (-도 means "not even")
- A는커녕 B조차 (-조차 means "not even" and makes the sentence more formal)
- A는커녕 B만 (-만 means "only" or "just")

Sample Sentences

학생들이 공부를 열심히 하기는커녕 수업에도 안 왔어요.

= Let alone study hard, the students did not even come to class.

= I was expecting the students to (at least) study hard, but they did not even do that. Rather, they did not even come to class.

칭찬받기는커녕 야단만 맞았어요.

= Let alone getting complimented, all I got was a scolding.

= Rather than being complimented, I actually only got scolded.

제 여동생은 주말에 집안일을 돕기는커녕, 거의 집에 있지도 않아요.

= My younger sister does not usually even stay at home on weekends, let alone help with chores.

돈이 남기는커녕 모자랐어요.

= Instead of having money left over, we did not even have enough.

저는 해외는커녕 서울 밖에도 안 나가 봤어요.

= Let alone overseas, I have never even been out of Seoul before.

숙제를 다 하기는커녕 시작조차 못 했어요.

= I could not even start the homework, much less finish it.

Alternative expressions

I. -은/는 고사하고

This expression can be used interchangeably with -은/는커녕 in most cases, and sounds more formal.

> **Ex)**
> 우승은커녕 예선 통과도 못 했어요.
> = Let alone winning, we did not even pass the preliminary round.
> = 우승은 고사하고 예선 통과도 못 했어요.
>
> 저는 비행기는커녕 아직 기차도 못 타 봤어요.
> = Let alone an airplane, I have never even taken a train.
> = 저는 비행기는 고사하고 아직 기차도 못 타 봤어요.

Track 35

When -은/는 고사하고 is used in the sense of "needless to mention (something)", its usage is different from -은/는커녕. For example, in the sentence, "그 사람은 일을 못하는 것은 고사하고, 일단 연락이 안 돼요", the expression -은/는 고사하고 means "before you even talk about (something)" or "not even discussing (a certain topic)". This usage is not found in -은/는커녕.

2. -은/는 물론이고, -뿐만 아니라

You can express a meaning similar to -은/는커녕 by using -은/는 물론이고 (= that is for sure, and...) or -뿐만 아니라 (= not only that, but also...). These two expressions have a wider range of usage than -은/는커녕, and you can list actions or states together that are not directly related. You can also list two positive things together.

Ex)

그 사람은 요리는 물론이고, 설거지도 안 해요.

= He does not even do the dishes, let alone cook.

저는 비행기뿐만 아니라 아직 기차도 못 타 봤어요.

= Let alone an airplane, I have never even taken a train.

3. -은/는 말할 것도 없고

-은/는 말할 것도 없고 means "there is not even anything to talk about" or "there is no reason to mention it". It is very similar to both -은/는 물론이고 and -뿐만 아니라.

Ex)

저는 비행기는 말할 것도 없고 아직 기차도 못 타 봤어요.

= Let alone an airplane, I have never even taken a train.

* Example of a positive sentence

그 사람은 노래는 말할 것도 없고 바이올린 연주도 잘해요.

= He is not only good at singing, but also good at playing the violin.

Grammatically incorrect but accepted sentences using -은/는커녕

Although it is grammatically incorrect, it is common for native Korean speakers to omit a verb when using -은/는커녕. For example, when saying that someone does not eat

134

a verb when using -은/는커녕. For example, when saying that someone does not eat vegetables "let alone" drink enough water, you are comparing 채소를 먹다 and 물을 충분히 마시다. The grammatically correct way to say this is, "그 사람은 채소를 먹기는커녕 물도 충분히 안 마셔요." However, people often omit the first verb, and say, "그 사람은 채소는커녕 물도 충분히 안 마셔요."

Technically, this sentence is incorrect because you cannot "drink" 채소. But even with one verb omitted, you can easily understand the sentence's intended meaning. For this reason, you will see a lot of grammatically incorrect sentences associated with -은/는커녕.

Track 35

135

Sample Dialogue

윤아: 보람 씨, 시험 잘 봤어요?

보람: 잘 보기는커녕 다 풀지도 못했어요.

윤아: 그렇게 어려웠어요?

보람: 네. 장학금은커녕 합격도 어려울 것
같아요.

Yoona: Boram, did you do well on the exam?

Boram: Rather than doing well, I couldn't even
solve all the questions.

Yoona: Was it that hard?

Boram: Yes. I'm not sure if I'll even pass, let alone
receive a scholarship.

✏ Exercises for Lesson 18

Complete each dialogue by using -은/는커녕 *to fill in the blank.*

Check the answers on **P. 233**

1.

A: 돈 좀 남았어요?

= Do you have some money left?

B: 네? ....:

= Pardon? Instead of having money left over, we did not even have enough.

2.

A: 숙제 다 했어요?

= Have you finished your homework?

B: ....:

= I could not even start the homework, much less finish it.

3.

A: 해외여행 가 봤어요?

= Have you ever traveled abroad?

B: ....:

= Let alone overseas, I have never even been out of Seoul before.

4.

A: 선생님한테 칭찬받았어요?

= Did you get a compliment from your teacher?

B: 네? ....

= Pardon? Let alone compliments, all I got was a scolding.

5.

A: 여동생이 주말에 집안일 많이 도와요?

= Does your younger sister help with chores on the weekends?

B: ....

= My younger sister does not usually even stay at home on weekends, let alone help with chores.

Check the answers on **p. 233**

LESSON **19**

Even if it means I have to

-아/어/여서라도

In Level 5 Lesson 15, we looked at the grammar point -(이)라도. This grammar point is used to suggest an idea that might not be the most ideal option, but can serve the purpose in the given situation.

Track
37

-아/어/여서라도 is simply a combination of -아/어/여서 (= by doing something) and -라도. It means "even if it is by doing" something or "even if I have to do" something, and describes doing something in order to achieve a desired outcome. This expression is commonly used and has a number of fixed phrases.

> ### *Conjugation*
> Verb stem + **-아/어/여서라도**

Sample Sentences

밤을 새워서라도 마무리할게요.

= I will finish it even if I have to stay up all night.

139

다른 약속을 취소해서라도 꼭 갈게요.

= I will be there for sure, even if I have to cancel other plans.

돈을 빌려서라도 살 거예요.

= I am going to buy it even if I have to borrow money.

지구 전체를 다 뒤져서라도 찾아낼 거예요.

= I will find it even if it means I have to search the entire planet.

Commonly used expressions

Track
37

I. 무슨 수를 써서라도 = no matter what I have to do

무슨 means "what kind of", and 수 means "method", "way", or "idea". 무슨 수를 써서라도 literally means "no matter what kind of method I have to use".

Ex)
무슨 수를 써서라도 다음에는 제가 우승할 거예요.

= No matter what I have to do, I will win first place next time.

2. 무슨 짓을 해서라도 = no matter what I have to do

짓, meaning "deed" or "behavior", is not a very respectful word. By saying 무슨 짓을 해서라도, you are expressing that you will achieve your goal "by doing whatever it takes", and that your actions will probably not be very nice or graceful.

Ex)

무슨 짓을 해서라도 복수할 거예요.

= I will get my revenge no matter what I have to do.

3. 어떻게 해서라도 = no matter what I have to do, whatever it takes

어떻게 해서라도 is a neutral expression. It literally means "even regardless of how I do it".

Ex)

어떻게 해서라도 다음 달까지 끝내 볼게요.

= No matter how I do it, I will try and finish it by next month.

4. 빚을 내서라도 = even if it is by getting a loan

Track
37

빚 means debt, and 빚을 내다 means to get a loan or to borrow money (usually a large amount). Even when you are not talking about actual debt or a loan, you often hear this expression used to emphasize how important something is to do or buy regardless of whether you can afford it or not.

Ex)

이런 건 빚을 내서라도 사야 돼요.

= Even if you have to get a loan, you need to buy this.

A different usage of -아/어/여서라도

In this lesson, we are looking at the usage of -아/어/여라도 that has the meaning of "even if it is by doing" so-and-so. However when -아/어/여서, which means "because", is combined

141

with -라도, the phrase can also take on the meaning of "at least because" or "at least for the reason of".

Ex)

저는 창피해서라도 그런 말 못 할 것 같아요.

= I do not think I would be able to say such a thing, at least out of embarrassment.

**Track
37**

Sample Dialogue

Track 38

승완: 벌써 네 시네. 희주야, 일이 아직도
　　　이렇게 많이 남았는데 이따가 콘서트 갈
　　　수 있을까?

희주: 갈 수 있어! 무슨 수를 써서라도 퇴근
　　　시간 전에 다 끝내자!

승완: 하... 아무리 생각해도 여섯 시까지는 못
　　　끝낼 것 같아. 그냥 콘서트 포기하자.

희주: 안 돼. 난 포기할 수 없어. 어떻게
　　　해서라도 꼭 갈 거야!

Seung-wan: It's already 4 o'clock. Heeju, we still have this much work left. Do you think we will be able to go to the concert later?

Heeju: We will! No matter what we have to do, let's finish everything before we clock out!

Seung-wan: Phew... No matter how much I think about it, I don't think we will be able to finish by 6. Let's just give up on the concert.

Heeju: No way. I can't give up. I will go no matter what.

143

✎ Exercises for Lesson 19

The following phrases mean "no matter what I have to do". Fill in the blanks.

1. 어떻게 ....

2. 무슨 .... 써서라도

3. 무슨 .... 해서라도

*The following phrases are commonly used phrases that use -***아/어/여서라도***. Fill in the blanks.*

4. 빚을 .... = even if it's by getting a loan

5. 밤을 .... = even if it's by staying up all night

6. 지구 전체를 다 .... = even if it's by searching the entire planet

LESSON **20**

Sentence Building Drill 19

Sentence Building Drill 19

In this series, we focus on how you can use the grammatical rules and expressions that you have previously learned to train yourself to comfortably make Korean sentences.

Track
39

We will start off with THREE key sentences and practice changing different parts of these sentences so that you do not end up simply memorizing the same three sentences. We want you to be able to make Korean sentences as flexibly as possible.

Key Sentence (1)

아까 거기는 공원이라기보다는 아이들이 노는 놀이터인 것 같던데요.

= That place earlier, rather than being a park, seemed more like a playground where kids play.

Key Sentence (2)

어제 컴퓨터가 갑자기 고장 나는 바람에 발표 준비는커녕 아무것도 못 했어요.

= As a result of my computer breaking down suddenly yesterday, I could not do anything, let alone prepare for the presentation.

145

Key Sentence (3)

회의가 곧 시작될 텐데 우리 회의에 늦지 않게 사무실로 돌아갈까요?

= I guess the meeting will start soon, so shall we go back to the office so that we are not late for the meeting?

Expansion & Variation Practice with Key Sentence (1)

0. Original sentence:

아까 거기는 공원이라기보다는 아이들이 노는 놀이터인 것 같던데요.

= That place earlier, rather than being a park, seemed more like a playground where kids play.

1.

아까 거기는 공원이라기보다는

= that place earlier, rather than being a park...

여기는 프랑스 음식점이라기보다는

= this place is, rather than a French restaurant...

이 책은 초보자용이라기보다는

= this book is, rather than being for beginners...

이 앱은 영상 편집 앱이라기보다는

= this app is, rather than a video editing app...

그 배우는 인기가 아주 많다기보다는

= that actor is, rather than being very popular...

2.

아이들이 노는 놀이터인 것 같던데요.

= It looked like it was a playground for kids.

문을 닫은 것 같던데요.

= It looked like it was closed.

146

무슨 사진관인 것 같던데요.

= It looked like some sort of photo studio.

피아노 학원인 것 같던데요.

= It looked like it was a piano school.

주연 씨 자리에 없는 것 같던데요.

= It looked like Jooyeon was not at her desk.

Expansion & Variation Practice with Key Sentence (2)

0. Original sentence:

어제 컴퓨터가 갑자기 고장 나는 바람에 발표 준비는커녕 아무것도 못 했어요.

= As a result of my computer breaking down suddenly yesterday, I could not do anything, let alone prepare for the presentation.

Track 39

1.

어제 컴퓨터가 갑자기 고장 나는 바람에

= as a result of the computer breaking down suddenly yesterday

어제 회사에 지갑을 놓고 오는 바람에

= as a result of leaving my wallet at the office yesterday

친구들이 소문을 내는 바람에

= as a result of my friends spreading a rumor

핸드폰을 실수로 초기화하는 바람에

= as a result of resetting my phone by mistake

노트북 충전기를 안 가져오는 바람에

= as a result of not bringing my laptop charger

147

2.

발표 준비는커녕 아무것도 못 했어요.

= I could not do anything, let alone prepare for the presentation.

선물은커녕 아무것도 못 샀어요.

= I could not buy anything, let alone a present.

저녁은커녕 점심도 못 먹었어요.

= I could not even have lunch, let alone dinner.

휴가를 가기는커녕 주말에도 못 쉬어요.

= I cannot even rest on the weekends, let alone go on vacation.

이름은커녕 얼굴도 기억이 안 나요.

= I do not even remember his face, let alone his name.

Expansion & Variation Practice with Key Sentence (3)

Track 39

0. Original sentence:

회의가 곧 시작될 텐데 우리 회의에 늦지 않게 사무실로 돌아갈까요?

= I guess the meeting will start soon, so shall we go back to the office so that we are not late for the meeting?

1.

회의가 곧 시작될 텐데

= I guess the meeting will start soon, so...

그렇게 앉으면 나중에 허리 아플 텐데

= if you sit like that, I think your back will hurt later, so...

갑자기 일정을 바꾸면 다른 사람들이 안 좋아할 텐데

= if you change the schedule suddenly, I guess other people will not like it, so...

그렇게 하면 더 비쌀 텐데

= it will become more expensive if you do it that way, so...

자꾸 그러면 들킬 텐데

= if you keep doing that, you will get caught, so...

2.

우리 회의에 늦지 않게 사무실로 돌아갈까요?

= Shall we go back to the office so that we are not late for the meeting?

나중에 헷갈리지 않게 지금 결정할까요?

= Shall we decide now so that we will not be confused later?

내일 바쁘지 않게 지금 해 놓을까요?

= Shall we do it now so that we will not be busy tomorrow?

아이들이 만지지 못하게 여기에 둘까요?

= Shall we put it here so that children cannot touch it?

다른 사람들이 볼 수 없게 여기에 숨길까요?

= Shall we hide it here so that other people will not be able to see it?

Track 39

Sample Dialogue

현우: 경화 씨, 아침 먹었어요?

경화: 아니요. 늦잠 자는 바람에 아침을 먹기는커녕 화장도 못 하고 나왔어요.

현우: 경화 씨가 늦잠을 잤어요?

경화: 네. 알람 맞추는 걸 깜빡했거든요.

현우: 내일은 아침 일찍 회의 있는 거 알죠? 늦잠 자지 않게 오늘 밤에 알람 꼭 맞추고 자요.

Hyunwoo: Kyung-hwa, did you have breakfast?

Kyung-hwa: No. Because I overslept, I couldn't even put on makeup before I left home, let alone have breakfast.

Hyunwoo: You overslept?

Kyung-hwa: Yes, because I forgot to set an alarm.

Hyunwoo: You know that there is a meeting early in the morning tomorrow, right? Make sure you set an alarm before you go to bed tonight so that you don't oversleep.

✐ Exercises for Lesson **20**

Check the answers on **p. 233**

Choose the statement that you CANNOT know by reading the quote.

1. 지나: "아까 거기는 공원이라기보다는 아이들이 노는 놀이터인 것 같던데요."

  ① 지나는 오늘 놀이터처럼 보이는 공원을 봤다.

  ② 지나는 공원과 놀이터는 다르다고 생각한다.

  ③ 지나의 말을 듣는 사람은 '거기'가 어디인지 알고 있다.

  ④ 지나는 오늘 놀이터에 갈 것이다.

2. 소희: "어제 컴퓨터가 갑자기 고장 나는 바람에 발표 준비는커녕 아무것도 못 했어요."

  ① 소희는 컴퓨터가 있다.

  ② 소희는 어제 발표 준비를 해야 했다.

  ③ 소희는 오늘 발표를 해야 한다.

  ④ 소희는 컴퓨터 때문에 아무것도 못 했다.

3. 예림: "회의가 곧 시작될 텐데 우리 회의에 늦지 않게 사무실로 돌아갈까요?"

  ① 예림은 지금 사무실에 있다.

  ② 예림은 오늘 회의에 참석해야 한다.

  ③ 예림의 말을 듣는 사람은 오늘 회의에 참석해야 한다.

  ④ 예림과 예림의 말을 듣는 사람은 사무실에 있다가 나왔다.

BLOG

Moving to Korea

You have made it to Level 10 of TTMIK, and at this point we might assume that you could be interested in visiting Korea or even moving here. If you are, that is fantastic, and you will get along just fine since you already know the language well.

I, myself, have been in Korea for over 10 years now and absolutely love it. When I first moved here, I never imagined that I would still be here years later. But I would not change a thing, as I have met some really cool people during my stay here.

But this blog is not about me. Instead, I would like to help make your move here as easy as possible. I will go into a few things you will need to prepare to get a visa and secure housing. So, let us get started.

Let us start with your visa. If you are planning on moving to Korea, you will need a visa that will allow you to live here legally. One of the easiest ways to get a visa is by working with a company in Korea that can sponsor your visa. If you plan on moving to Korea to attend a university, you can also get a student visa sponsored by your school. Now, I moved here from the United States so some of the things you need might be different depending on the country you are from. So, think of this as a good starting point for what you need to prepare and do to move here.

I actually applied for my visa while I was still in the US after I was hired by a company in Korea. I went to the nearest Korean consulate in my state and had an interview. Once I passed the interview, I was able to move to Korea and begin working. So, what are some things you will need to get a visa? You will need identification, a photo, your passport, and the application fee. The company you work for will also have to prepare some documents, but they will give those to you or may even accompany you to the immigration office. There will also be a fee that you will have to pay. After getting your visa, you will also have to get your Alien Registration Card, or ARC. Again, you will need a photo, your passport, the application, and the fee.

Now, when you are at the immigration office, you will not hand cash to the person at the window. Instead, you have to purchase stamps from within the immigration office to use to get your ID card. Once the process is complete, you can either pay a small fee to have the card delivered to you, or you can come back when they call you to let you know your card is ready. And that is really all there is to it to register as an alien here in Korea. Just make sure you have the right paperwork and materials and it should go smoothly.

Let us talk about housing now. If you move here with a company, it is more than likely that they will have a place set up for you so you will not have to worry about finding a house. They might set you up with a villa, an apartment, or an officetel (a studio apartment). Oftentimes these will be one room flats, but sometimes they can be a bit different depending on the company you work for. If you decide that you want to look for your own place, you need to know that most places ask for "key" money, which is a very large deposit. The more the deposit, the less you pay in monthly rent. If you can afford to put down a large amount for the deposit up front, you can even get away with no monthly rent payments.

Let us break these two types of housing payments.

1. Jeonse (전세) - In this case, you will pay one very large sum up front but will not have any monthly rent payments. Typically, the rental contract will be for two years, but you can negotiate with the owner a little bit. Once the contract is up, you can either decide to

move out or sign a new contract with your landlord. It is at this point that the landlord can also decide if they want to increase the amount of your deposit. When you move out, the landlord will return the entire deposit to you.

2. Wolse (월세) - In this agreement, you will pay a certain amount up front as a deposit as well as monthly rent during your contract. Sometimes you can negotiate with the landlord to pay more up front for a cheaper monthly rent, and sometimes they will even let you pay less up front for a more expensive monthly rent payment.

These are the two main types of housing payments here in Korea. You can find some places where you can pay month-to-month, or some where you can pay the entire amount up front for however long you plan on staying. However, these types of arrangements are not that common in Korea.

Let us talk about your visa type and a few tips I have learned while living here. Each visa type is different and allows you to do certain things. A tourist visa allows you to stay in Korea for an extended amount of time, but you cannot work. There are also various types of work visas. For example, an E-2 visa allows you to teach in Korea. With an E-2 visa, you are only allowed to work for the school that sponsors your visa. If you marry a Korean, you can apply for an F-visa which will allow you to work in just about any field. There are also other ways to get a permanent visa that allows more freedom in what types of jobs you can have. There is a program called KIIP, which is a Korean language program that helps obtain a permanent visa. If that is something you might be interested in, I highly suggest looking up KIIP and beginning right away on trying to earn a permanent visa.

Obviously, these are not the only types of visas. I suggest checking out www.immigration.go.kr for more information on each visa type to find one that is right for you.

A lot of these visas will last for one year. After one year, you will be sent a letter in the mail to let you know you need to renew your visa if you plan on staying. You will need to make an appointment with the immigration office on their website. Then, just like when you first received your ID, you will need a photo, the application form, your passport, your current ARC, and the fee.

One thing I learned (the hard way) is to be sure to report any changes in address or passport information. I had to renew my passport and forgot to report it to immigration. Once I remembered, I went to the office and filled out the forms to let them know about the change. Since I was late, I was charged a pretty hefty fee, but I was told if I had waited a bit longer, it would have been even worse. So, learn from my mistake. Any time you change your address in Korea or renew any of your identification, be sure to head over to the immigration office as soon as you can.

And welcome to Korea! I hope this has provided you with a bit of helpful information about what you will need to stay here in Korea.

Written by Johnny Bland

LESSON 21

Advanced Idiomatic Expressions 14

말 (Word)

Track
41

This is an Advanced Idiomatic Expressions lesson related to 말, which means "word(s)" or "language". In order to fully understand and use the expressions introduced in this series, it is essential that you understand the grammatical structure of the sentences. When you come across a grammar point that you are unfamiliar with, please go back and review the related TTMIK lessons.

Keyword: **말** = word(s), language, what one says

1. 말을 높이다 = to speak in formal language to someone

높다 means "to be high", and 높이다 means "to make something higher" or "to raise" something. Therefore 말을 높이다 means to speak in 존댓말, with respect and formality. It is usually used in a negative form to tell someone that they can feel free to speak in 반말 to you. The act of starting to speak in 반말 to someone is 말을 놓다, so you can say "말 놓으세요" to someone who is unnecessarily speaking 존댓말 to you.

158

Ex)

저한테는 말 안 높이셔도 돼요. 말 편하게 하세요.

= You do not have to speak formally to me. Please speak in casual language to me.

2. 말도 안 되다 = to not make sense; to be nonsensical

되다 means "to become", so if you say 말이 안 되다, it literally means "it does not become a word/language". When you experience something ridiculous, and you think it is nonsensical, you can say "말이 안 돼요". If you add -도, which means "even", and say 말도 안 되다, it means "to not even make sense" and makes the meaning of the sentence stronger. On the contrary, if you would like to say that something does make sense, you can just say 말이 되다. However, please note that using 도 with 말이 되다 sounds unnatural.

Track 41

Ex)

말도 안 돼. 한국어 한 달 배우고 토픽 6급을 땄다는 게 말이 돼?

= Impossible. Does it make sense that he/she passed TOPIK level 6 after learning Korean for a month?

3. 말을 아끼다 = to save one's breath, to not say much

아끼다 means to save or cherish something so that it is not wasted. So 말을 아끼다 means that there are definitely things you could say, but you choose not to speak much on the matter. This is usually done to avoid unnecessary trouble or interest from other people.

Ex)

저도 하고 싶은 말은 많았지만, 오늘 기자들 앞에서는 말을 아꼈습니다.

= I had a lot that I wanted to say, too, but in front of the reporters today, I did not say much.

4. 말이 많다 = to be talkative; there is considerable controversy (over something)

많다 means "to be a lot", so 말이 많다 can simply mean that someone is talkative. However, if you describe a thing or an event as 말이 많다, it means that there is a lot of controversy over the thing or the event. You can imagine a situation where a lot of people are criticizing something.

Ex)
요즘 그 회사에 대해서 말이 많아요.
= There is a lot of controversy about that company these days.

Track 41

5. 말이 통하다 = to understand each other well, to click

통하다 means "to connect" or "to go through". When 말이 잘 통하다 is used to describe two people, it means that they can relate to each other well and are on the same wavelength. When you describe someone as a 말이 통하는 사람, it means that they understand what you say, and you can have good conversations with them.

Ex)
오랜만에 말이 통하는 친구를 만나서 너무 좋아요.
= I am so happy to have made a new friend that I can have good conversations with for the first time in a while.

6. 말이 안 통하다 = to be unreasonable, to be ridiculous

말이 통하다 is used to talk about two or more people who click well with and understand one another. However, 말이 안 통하다 refers to a person who is difficult to talk to because they are unreasonable or ridiculous. If you say 말이 안 통하다 about two people not understanding each other, the context is usually about not speaking the other person's native language.

Ex)
말이 통해야 이야기를 하지... 그 사람이랑은 도무지 말이 안 통해요.
= To have a conversation, you need to mutually understand each other. He is just unreasonable. You cannot talk to him.

Track 41

7. 말문이 막히다 = to be at a loss for words, to be speechless

말문 literally means "word door" and refers to your mouth, and 막히다 means "to be blocked". You never refer to your mouth as 말문 on its own, but the idiomatic phrase 말문이 막히다 is used quite commonly when you do not know what to say because you are shocked or overwhelmed.

Ex)
갑작스러운 제안에 너무 놀라서 말문이 막혔어요.
= I was so surprised by the sudden offer that I did not know what to say.

8. 말을 꺼내다 = to bring up a topic

꺼내다 means "to take something out" or "to pull something out". Imagine pulling words out of your head that you have had for a while. It can be used to refer to both heavy topics that you have been hesitating to mention or light topics that you are briefly mentioning.

Ex)
저도 오랫동안 고민하다가 어렵게 말을 꺼낸 거예요.
= I also hesitated for a long time before I brought it up with difficulty.

9. **말 나오지 않게 하다** = to prevent people from talking about something, to not let others complain about something

말이 나오다 literally means "words come out". It is often used to mean that people are talking about something negative, and either complaining about it or criticizing it. For example, if you play the drums at midnight every night, and your neighbors start talking about it, you can use the expression 말이 나오다 to describe your neighbors. This expression is often used in the form 말이 나오지 않게, which means "so that people do not criticize it".

Ex)
더 이상 말 나오지 않게 앞으로 더 조심하세요.
= Be careful so that there will not be any more talk about it in the future.

10. **말이 아니다** = to be in a terrible situation, to be in an unspeakable condition

The literal translation of 말이 아니다 can be misleading, but what it actually means is 말할 수 있는 상태가 아니다 (= to not be in a situation that can be spoken of). When a situation or condition is so bad that you cannot even talk about it, you can say 말이 아니다.

Ex)

지금은 정말 상황이 말이 아니에요.

= Right now the situation is really terrible.

11. 말이 말 같지 않다 = to not be worth listening to

Literally translated, 말이 말 같지 않다 means "words do not sound like words". When someone's words or remarks are so ridiculous that they seem like noise or meaningless sound, you can use the expression 말 같지 않다. Other variations are "말 같은 소리를 해야지 (= You need to say something that makes sense, not this current nonsense)", "말 같지 않은 소리 그만해 (= Stop talking nonsense)", "and 사람 말이 말 같지 않아? (= You think that what I am saying is not worth listening to?)" These expressions are often said in 반말 because they are not very respectful expressions to begin with.

Track
41

Ex)

내 말이 말 같지 않아? 왜 자꾸 그러는 거야?

= Do you think what I am saying is worthless? Why do you keep doing that?

12. 입에 발린 말을 하다 = to pay lip service, to flatter

바르다 means to apply something, like lotion or cream, on a surface. 입에 발린 말 literally means "words that are coated on the mouth" or "words that are applied on the mouth" and refers to lip service or flattering words that may not necessarily be true.

Ex)

그 사람은 맨날 입에 발린 말만 해요. 다 믿으면 안 돼요.

= He always only pays lip service. You should not believe everything he says.

163

13. **할 말을 잃다** = to be at a loss for words, to not know what to say

잃다 means "to lose", and 할 말을 잃다 means that you are lost for words and do not know what to say. You usually use this expression when talking about something absurd or hard to believe. 할 말을 잃다 often also carries the connotation of "giving up" or "not even trying to persuade otherwise" because the other person's behavior or remarks are so ridiculous.

Ex)

그 사람이 너무 뻔뻔하게 나와서 제가 할 말을 잃었어요.

= He acted so shamelessly that I was at a loss for words.

Track 41

Sample Dialogue

현우: 경화 씨, 석진 씨한테 요즘 무슨 일
　　　있냐고 물어봤어요?

경화: 네. 근데 말을 꺼내기가 무섭게 아무 일
　　　없다고 하더라고요.

현우: 진짜요? 아무 일 없대요?

경화: 네. 저한테는 말을 아끼는 것 같아요.
　　　현우 씨가 한번 이야기해 봐요.

현우: 네, 그럴게요.

Hyunwoo: Kyung-hwa, did you ask Seokjin if
　　　something is going on with him these
　　　days?

Kyung-hwa: Yes, but as soon as I brought it up, he
　　　said that nothing happened to him.

Hyunwoo: Really? He said nothing happened?

Kyung-hwa: Yes. I think he's not saying much to me.
　　　You should try talking to him.

Hyunwoo: Okay, I will.

✐ Exercises for Lesson 21

Fill in the blanks with the appropriate idioms with 말 *from this lesson.*

Check the answers on **p. 234**

1. (   )

    = to pay lip service, to flatter

2. (   )

    = to speak in formal language to someone

3. (   )

    = to bring up a topic

4. (   )

    = to understand each other well, to click

5. (   )

    = to save one's breath, to not say much

The Final Step in Talk To Me In Korean's

LESSON **22**

Various Usages of the Ending -며

> # -며

In this lesson, we are going to look at the suffix -며, which can be used for a variety of purposes, including connecting two nouns or verbs. When connecting nouns, -(으)며 is used, and when connecting verbs, -(이)며 is used.

Track 43

> ### Conjugation
>
> Verb stem + -(으)며
> Noun + -(이)며

Usage 1

-(으)며 can be used to connect two verbs in a parallel manner. It is interchangeable with -고, and is often used to replace -고 to avoid repetition in sentences. It is less commonly used in daily conversation and used more often in formal speech and written Korean.

167

Ex)

이 컴퓨터는 가볍고, 빠르며, 가격이 높지 않아요.

= This computer is light, fast, and inexpensive.

= 이 컴퓨터는 가볍고, 빠르고, 가격이 높지 않아요.

이 방법은 간편하고, 효과가 좋으며, 누구나 사용할 수 있어요.

= This method is simple and effective, and can be used by anyone.

= 이 방법은 간편하고, 효과가 좋고, 누구나 사용할 수 있어요.

Usage 2

Track 43

You can also use -(으)며 to connect two actions that are happening at the same time, with the meaning of "while doing something". It is mostly interchangeable with -(으)면서, but -(으)며 sounds more formal in most cases. One difference between -(으)면서 and -(으)며, however, is that -(으)면서 can be used to mean "even though", but -(으)며 cannot.

Ex)

아이들은 웃으며 사진을 찍었어요.

= The kids took photos while laughing.

= 아이들은 웃으면서 사진을 찍었어요.

저는 커피를 마시며 책 읽는 걸 좋아해요.

= I like to read a book while drinking coffee.

= 저는 커피를 마시면서 책 읽는 걸 좋아해요.

손님이 지갑을 꺼내며 물었습니다. "얼마예요?"

= The customer asked as he pulled out his wallet, "How much is it?"

= 손님이 지갑을 꺼내면서 물었습니다. "얼마예요?"

Usage 3

When connecting nouns, -(이)며 is used instead of -(으)며. However, the usage of -(이)며 is quite different from other words that mean "and" in Korean. The most common words for listing things are -하고, -와/과, -(이)랑 and 그리고. These words are used to mention a limited number of items, like "A and B" or "A, B, and C".

But when -(이)며 is used to list nouns, its usage implies that not every existing item is being mentioned, and that there are likely more that could be mentioned.

Examples

Track 43

I.

책이며 공책이며 바닥에 다 떨어져 있었어요.

= Things like books and notebooks were all on the floor.

책이랑 공책이랑 바닥에 다 떨어져 있었어요.

= Books and notebooks were all on the floor.

* -(이)며 tends to be used in repetition, after each noun that is mentioned, just like -(이)랑.

2.

얼마 전에 이사를 했는데, 식탁이며 의자며 아직도 살 게 많아요.

= I moved recently, and I still have a lot of things to buy, like a kitchen table, chairs, etc.

얼마 전에 이사를 했는데, 식탁이랑 의자를 사야 돼요.

= I moved recently, and I need to buy a kitchen table and chairs.

Please also note that if you see -이며 after what seems like a verb, it is because the verb's verb stem ends with -이. For example, the verb 움직이다 changes to 움직이며.

169

Sample Dialogue

Track 44

석진: 승완 씨, 가방 산다고 했죠? 이 가방은 어때요?

승완: 아... 별로 튼튼해 보이지 않네요. 저는 책이며 노트북이며 들고 다니는 게 많거든요.

석진: 그렇군요. 그럼 이 가방은 어때요? 가볍고, 튼튼하며, 가격도 합리적이라고 쓰여 있어요.

승완: 오! 딱 제가 찾는 가방이네요. 감사해요.

* 딱 = *exactly*

** 합리적이다 = *to be reasonable*

Seokjin: Seung-wan, you said you wanted to buy a bag, right? What do you think of this bag?

Seung-wan: Ah... It doesn't really look sturdy. I carry around a lot of things like books, my laptop, and other stuff.

Seokjin: I see. Then, how about this bag? It says that it is light, sturdy, and reasonably priced.

Seung-wan: Oh! That's exactly the bag I've been looking for. Thank you.

✏ Exercises for Lesson **22**

Fill in the blanks using –(으)며 *or* –(이)며.

1. 손님이 지갑을 (   ) 물었습니다. "얼마예요?"

  = 손님이 지갑을 꺼내면서 물었습니다. "얼마예요?"

2. 아이들은 (   ) 사진을 찍었어요.

  = 아이들은 웃으면서 사진을 찍었어요.

3. 이 컴퓨터는 가볍고, (   ), 가격이 높지 않아요.

  = 이 컴퓨터는 가볍고, 빠르고, 가격이 높지 않아요.

4. 이 방법은 간편하고, 효과가 (   ), 누구나 사용할 수 있어요.

  = 이 방법은 간편하고, 효과가 좋고, 누구나 사용할 수 있어요.

5. 얼마 전에 이사를 했는데, (   ) 아직도 살 게 많아요.

  = I moved recently, and I still have a lot of things to buy, like a kitchen table, chairs, etc.

6. (   ) 바닥에 다 떨어져 있었어요.

  = Things like books and notebooks were all on the floor.

Check the answers on **p. 234**

171

LESSON **23**

Maybe because

-아/어/여서인지

Track
45

In this lesson, we are going to take a look at how to say "maybe because..." in Korean. The structure you use to say this is -아/어/여서인지 and is comprised of -아/어/여서 combined with -인지.

-아/어/여서 = because

-인지 = whether or not

In this structure, the phrase 모르겠지만 (= I do not know but) is actually an omitted phrase after -인지. So in full, the structure is -아/어/여서인지 모르겠지만 (= I do not know if it is because ... but), but 모르겠지만 is very commonly dropped. In addition to 모르겠지만, other similar phrases may be omitted in the same way, such as 확실하지 않지만 (= it is not certain but), 정확히 알 수 없지만 (= cannot know exactly but), and more.

Ex)

일요일이어서인지* 사람이 많네요.

= Maybe because it is a Sunday, there are a lot of people.

* 일요일이어서인지 = 일요일이다 + -아/어/여서인지

Original form

일요일이어서인지 모르겠지만, 사람이 많네요.

= I do not know if it is because it is a Sunday, but there are a lot of people.

Variations

1. 그래서인지 = maybe because of that

   Ex)

   그래서인지 오늘 기분이 안 좋아 보이더라고요.

   = Maybe because of that, he did not seem to be in a good mood today.

   * 그래서인지 is often shortened to 그래선지, especially in colloquial situations.

Track
45

2. 어쩌면 -아/어/여서인지 = maybe because...
(어쩌면 = maybe, perhaps)

   Ex)

   어쩌면 너무 많이 떨어뜨려서인지 제 휴대폰이 갑자기 안 켜져요.

   = Maybe because I dropped it too much, my phone suddenly will not turn on.

3. -아/어/여서인지 몰라도 = I do not know if it is because... but

   Ex)

   모임 장소가 너무 멀어서인지 몰라도, 참가자가 적었어요.

   = I do not know if it was because the meetup place was too far away, but there were not many participants.

Alternative expressions

1. -기 때문인지 = maybe because...

Instead of using -아/어/여서 to mean "because", you can also use -기 때문 + -인지 to express almost the same meaning.

> **Ex)**
> 잠을 너무 많이 자서인지 허리가 아파요.
> = 잠을 너무 많이 잤기 때문인지 허리가 아파요.
> = Maybe because I slept too much, my lower back is aching.

2. -아/어/여서 그런지 = maybe because...

If you add 그렇다 to -인지 to form 그런지, the expression becomes -아/어/여서 그런지. This does not change the overall meaning of the sentence, but just makes the sentence a little softer and more colloquial. -아/어/여서 그렇다 literally means "it is like that because..."

> **Ex)**
> 아까 콜라를 너무 많이 마셔서인지 배가 아파요.
> = 아까 콜라를 너무 많이 마셔서 그런지 배가 아파요.
> = Maybe because I drank too much cola earlier, my stomach hurts.

Sample Sentences
오늘 커피를 너무 많이 마셔서인지 잠이 잘 안 와요.
= Maybe because I had too much coffee today, I cannot sleep.

날씨가 좋아서인지 바닷가에 가고 싶어졌어요.

= Maybe because the weather is good, now I feel like going to the ocean.

살이 좀 빠져서인지 더 젊어 보여요.

= Maybe because you have lost some weight, you look younger.

제가 어제 잠을 많이 못 자서인지 오늘은 공부에 집중이 안 돼요.

= Maybe because I did not sleep well last night, I cannot focus on studying today.

바람이 많이 불어서인지 어제보다 추운 것 같아요.

= Maybe because it is very windy, it feels like it is colder than yesterday.

Track
45

175

Sample Dialogue

준배: 평일이어서 그런지 영화관에 사람이
없네요.

다혜: 그러게요. 어, 영화 시작한다.

준배: 근데... 다혜 씨... 사람이 없어서인지
좀 무섭네요.

다혜: 어! 저기 귀신 있다!

준배: 으악!

*Joonbae: Maybe because it's a weekday, there are
not a lot of people in the theater.*

Dahye: Right. Oh, the movie is starting.

*Joonbae: But... Dahye... Maybe because there are
not a lot of people, it's a bit scary.*

Dahye: Oh, there's a ghost over there!

Joonbae: Yikes!

✏ *Exercises for Lesson 23*

Translate each sentence into Korean using **–아/어/여서인지** *and write it on the lines provided.*

I. Maybe because you have lost some weight, you look younger.

....

2. Maybe because I had too much coffee today, I cannot sleep.

....

3. Maybe because the weather is good, now I feel like going to the ocean.

....

4. Maybe because it is very windy, it feels like it is colder than yesterday.

....

5. Maybe because I did not sleep well last night, I cannot focus on studying today.

....

Check the answers on **p. 234**

177

LESSON 24

I guess I will have to

-아/어/여야겠다

Track
47

In this lesson, we are going to look at the commonly used sentence ending -아/어/여야겠다. This structure is used to say things like "I guess I will have to…" or "I need to…" to make an assumption about what needs to be done. In order to fully understand -아/어/여야겠다, you need to understand -겠- well first, which was first covered in Level 6 Lesson 16. We will briefly review it below.

Understanding -겠-

You can use -겠- to express your own assumption or intention, or to ask someone about theirs. You can commonly see -겠- in fixed expressions such as, "잘 먹겠습니다 (= Thanks for the food. / Let's eat. / I will enjoy the food.)" or, "알겠습니다 (= I see. / I understand what you are saying.)" It is also frequently used to talk about what you are willing to do, like when you say, "제가 하겠습니다! (= I will do it. / Let me do it.)"

Construction

-아/어/여야겠다 is a combination of -아/어/여야 하다 and -겠-, and is frequently used when talking to yourself, as well as when talking to someone else.

- -아/어/여야 하다 = to have to

- -겠- = show of assumption/intention

  → 아/어/여야겠다 = I guess I will have to; it looks like I need to; I understand that I should

Understanding -아/어/여야겠다

-아/어/여야겠다 is used not only to express "I guess I will have to" in the literal sense, but also to express what you think needs to be done after seeing something or getting new information. When used in the latter sense, the meaning is often not translated but rather is understood through context. -아/어/여야겠다 is also only used with action verbs.

Track
47

Sample Sentences (when talking to someone else)

우리도 서둘러야겠어요.

= (I guess) we should hurry up, too.

다시 확인해 봐야겠어요.

= (I guess) I will have to check again.

품절되기 전에 빨리 주문해야겠어요.

= (I guess) we will have to order it quickly before it is sold out.

179

한 시간 정도 기다려야겠어요.

= We will have to wait for about an hour.

차 막히기 전에 출발해야겠어요.

= We will have to leave before the traffic gets bad.

Sample Sentences (when you are talking to yourself)

잠깐 쉬어야겠다.

= I need to take a break for a little while.

나중에 먹어야겠다.

= I am going to eat it later.

Track 47

나도 이거 사야겠다.

= I need to buy this, too.

이제 집에 가야겠다.

= I need to go home now.

-지 말아야겠다

Earlier in this lesson, you learned that -아/어/여야겠다 can be used to express what you think needs to be done after seeing something or getting new information. On the other hand, to express what you think should not be done, you can use -지 말아야겠다. This is a combination of -지 말다 and -아/어/여야겠다. You could also say 안 -아/어/여야겠다 or -지 않아야겠다 for the same meaning, but -지 말아야겠다 is more commonly used.

Sample Sentences

이제 플라스틱 빨대를 쓰지 말아야겠어요.

= I think I should stop using plastic straws now.

앞으로는 6시에 퇴근하지 말아야겠어요.

= I think I should not leave work at 6 o'clock from now on.

밤늦게 뭘 먹지 말아야겠다.

= I think I should not eat late at night.

너무 무리하지 말아야겠다.

= I think I should not work too hard/go overboard.

**Track
47**

Sample Dialogue

Track
48

동근: 보람 씨, 보람 씨는 커피 안 마시죠? 먼저
들어가세요. 저는 커피 좀 사 가지고
들어가야겠어요.

보람: 커피요? 커피 끊겠다면서요.

동근: 안 되겠어요. 머리가 너무 아파서 한 잔
마셔야겠어요.

보람: 그래요? 그럼 같이 사러 가요.

Dong-geun: Boram, you don't drink coffee, right?
You go ahead. I think I'll buy some coffee
before going in.

Boram: Coffee? You said you would quit drinking
coffee.

Dong-geun: I don't think I can. My head really
hurts, so I think I need to drink a cup.

Boram: Really? Then let's go buy some together.

The Final Step in Talk To Me In Korean's

✏️ *Exercises for Lesson* **24**

Translate each sentence into Korean using **–아/어/여야겠어요** *or* **–아/어/여야겠다** *and write it on the lines provided.*

(When talking to someone)

1. (I guess) we should hurry up, too.

....

2. We will have to leave before the traffic gets bad.

....

3. I think I should stop using plastic straws now.

....

(When talking to yourself)

4. I need to go home now.

....

5. I am going to eat it later.

....

6. I think I should not eat late at night.

....

Check the answers on **p. 234**

183

LESSON 25

To be bound to

-기/게 마련이다

In this lesson, we are going to look at an expression you can use to talk about something that happens all the time or has a very strong tendency to happen. The main word for this expression is 마련, and it is used in the form of "verb stem + **-기 마련이다**" or "verb stem + **-게 마련이다**".

> ### Conjugation
> Verb stem + **-기/게 마련이다**

The full expression -기/게 마련이다 can be translated to "to be bound to", "to be prone to", "to be expected to", or "to be natural that it happens". Although the expression can be translated to "to be bound to", -기/게 마련이다 does not mean that something will "definitely" happen. Rather, it means that something has the potential to happen, but also might not happen. You can use either -기 or -게 before 마련이다, but -기 is more common.

The word 마련 is also used in the verb 마련하다, which means "to prepare" or "to prepare and obtain" something, like 대책을 마련하다 (= to come up with a countermeasure), 음식을 마련하다 (= to prepare food), and 집을 마련하다 (= to buy a house to live in). Be careful not to mix up these two different ways 마련 is used. In this lesson, we will focus only on the structure -기/게 마련이다.

Examples

좋은 일이 생기기 마련이에요.
= Good things are bound to happen.

결국 진실은 드러나기 마련이에요.
= The truth is bound to come to light eventually.

그럴 때가 있기 마련이에요.
= You are bound to have such times.

Track
49

Alternative expressions

To express a similar meaning, you can also say -게 되어 있어요 (= it is bound to be like that; it is designed to be that way; it is supposed to be like that) or -(으)ㄹ 가능성이 커요 (= there is a big possibility that...; it is likely that...). The structure -게 되어 있다 was also covered in Level 7 Lesson 25.

Examples

좋은 일이 생기게 마련이에요.
= Good things are bound to happen.

= 좋은 일이 생기게 되어 있어요.

= 좋은 일이 생길 가능성이 커요.

결국 진실은 드러나게 마련이에요.

= The truth is bound to come to light eventually.

= 결국 진실은 드러나게 되어 있어요.

= 결국 진실은 드러날 가능성이 커요.

Using -다 보면 with -기/게 마련이다

Track 49

Since -기/게 마련이다 is used to talk about the high probably or strong tendency of something happening, the expression -다 보면 is commonly used together with it. "Verb + -다 보면" means "when you do something for a while" or "as you do something, you will experience so-and-so."

Sample Sentences

사업을 하다 보면 어려움이 있기 마련이에요.

= When you run a business, you are bound to have difficulties (from time to time).

살다 보면 후회하는 일이 있기 마련이에요.

= As you live your life, there are certainly things you regret.

축구를 하다 보면 다치기 마련이죠.

= When you play soccer, you are bound to get hurt from time to time.

여러 사람이 같이 일을 하다 보면 오해가 있기 마련이에요.

= When several people work together, there will sometimes be misunderstandings.

The structure -(으)면 -기/게 마련이다 is also commonly used.

Sample Sentences

준비 운동을 안 하면 다치기 마련이에요.

= If you don't warm up before exercising, you are bound to get hurt.

시간이 지나면 잊혀지기 마련이에요.

= As time passes, it is bound to be forgotten.

> * 잊혀지다 is technically grammatically incorrect because two types of passive verb endings, -히- and -아/어/여지다, are being used together in one word. The correct form of the word to use is 잊히다. However, as covered in Level 6 Lesson 21, people tend to use this kind of "double passive voice" with certain verbs even though it is grammatically incorrect.

Track
49

Sample Dialogue

Track
50

예지: 승완 씨, 첫 촬영 어땠어요?

승완: 너무 긴장해서 무슨 말을 했는지 모르겠어요. 휴...

예지: 힘내요! 처음에는 누구나 긴장하기 마련이잖아요.

승완: 고마워요. 점점 나아지겠죠?

예지: 당연하죠. 계속 하다 보면 늘기 마련이에요.

Yeji: Seung-wan, how was your first shoot?

Seung-wan: I was so nervous that I don't remember what I said. Phew...

Yeji: Cheer up! Everyone is bound to get nervous at first.

Seung-wan: Thanks. I should get better gradually, right?

Yeji: Sure thing. As you keep doing it, you are bound to get better at it.

✏ *Exercises for Lesson 25*

Rewrite the following sentences using **-기 마련이다** *to have the same meaning as the sentence given.*

1. 축구를 하다 보면 다치게 되어 있어요.

→ ....

2. 시간이 지나면 잊혀지게 되어 있어요.

→ ....

3. 공부는 정말 필요하면 열심히 하게 되어 있어요.

→ ....

4. 아무리 게을러도, 손님이 오면 집 청소를 하게 되어 있어요.

→ ....

5. 영원한 비밀은 없어요. 사람들이 다 알게 되어 있어요.

→ ....

6. 재미있게 공부하면 성적도 좋아지게 되어 있어요.

→ ....

Check the answers on **p. 234**

LESSON **26**

Advanced Idiomatic Expressions 15

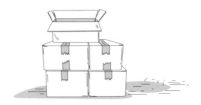

하나 (One)

Track
51

This is an Advanced Idiomatic Expressions lesson related to 하나, which means "one". In order to fully understand and use the expressions introduced in this series, it is essential that you understand the grammatical structure of the sentences. When you come across a grammar point that you are unfamiliar with, please go back and review the related TTMIK lessons.

Keyword: 하나 = one

1. 하나도 모르다
= to not know anything

-도 usually means "also" or "too" in positive sentences, but when used in a negative expression, it can also mean "not even". So 하나도 모르다 means "to not even know one" and therefore can be understood as "to know nothing".

190

Ex)

뭐가 뭔지 하나도 모르겠어요.

= I have no idea what is going on.

= I have no idea what is what. (I am confused.)

2. 하나도 없다

= to not have any, there is none

The literal translation of 하나도 없다 is "there is not even one", so the meaning of the phrase is that there is no amount of something. You can use this expression to talk about both things you can count, like 의자가 하나도 없어요 (= There are no chairs) and things you cannot count, like 돈이 하나도 없어요 (= I have no money at all). For things that are countable, you can replace 하나도 with 한 개도 to sound more casual.

Track
51

Ex)

세상에 쉬운 일이 하나도 없네요.

= There is nothing easy in this world.

3. 하나 없다

= to not have any, there is none, one is missing

하나 없다 and 하나도 없다 may look similar and can be translated similarly, but their usages are different. One difference is that 하나 없다 can be used to mean "one is missing", like 여기 컵 하나 없어요 (= We lack one cup here). However, the idiomatic usage of 하나 없다 in a negative sentence is even more interesting. With 하나도 없다, the subject that comes before 하나도 usually has a subject marking particle, like 연필이 하나도 없어요 (= As for pencils, I

191

do not have any), which creates a longer pause and time to anticipate the following phrase. However, 하나 없다 is shorter and is therefore more closely attached to the subject, often with the subject marker omitted. 하나 없다 is also often changed into the modifier form of 하나 없는, like 주름 하나 없는 피부 (= skin without even a single wrinkle).

Ex)

창문 하나 없는 사무실에서 일하고 싶지 않아요.

= I do not want to work in an office without even a single window.

4. 하나도 안 아프다

= to not hurt at all

Because the amount of pain one feels is not countable, the expression 하나도 안 is used to mean "not even one" or "not even a small bit". Therefore 하나도 안 아프다 means "to not hurt at all".

Ex)

다행히 매트 위에 떨어져서 하나도 안 아팠어요.

= Luckily, I fell onto the mattress so it did not hurt at all.

5. 하나도 남김없이

= without leaving anything, without anything left over, completely

남기다 means to leave something behind or to not finish something, like food or homework. 남김 is the noun form of the word and by adding -없이 after it, 남김없이 takes on the meaning of "without anything left". 하나도 남김없이 is used to describe something that is done or should be done thoroughly and completely.

Ex)

하나도 남김없이 저 방으로 옮기세요.

= Move everything to that room, without leaving anything behind.

6. 하나밖에 없는

= one and only, one of a kind

-밖에 없다 means to "only have" something, and 하나밖에 없다 means "to only have one". This expression is often used in the modifier form of 하나밖에 없는 to mean "one and only" or "one of a kind". For example, "세상에 하나밖에 없는 가방이에요" means, "This bag is one of a kind" or more literally, "There is only one bag like this in the world."

Track
51

Ex)

하나밖에 없는 오빠한테 이럴 거야?

= I am your one and only brother and you are going to do this to me?

7. 만에 하나

= by any possibility, out of a low probability

만 means ten thousand, so 만에 하나 literally means "one out of ten thousand (cases)". When something is considered highly unlikely but you want to mention the probability of it happening, you can say 만에 하나 to emphasize the meaning of "if" or "so, what if?"

Ex)

만에 하나 그날 갑자기 비가 오면 어떡해요?

= I know it is unlikely, but what if it suddenly rains that day?

193

8. 하나만 알고 둘은 모르다

= to only know one thing and not more, to know only one side of the whole story

When someone only considers one thing and fails to see beyond it, you can use this expression. It is usually used when the speaker can see the bigger picture.

Ex)

애들은 정말 하나만 알고 둘은 모른다니까. 숙제 다 하면 아이스크림 주려고 했는데.

= Kids really cannot see beyond what is right in front of them. I was going to give them ice cream once they finished their homework.

9. 하나부터 열까지

= from A to Z, every little detail, through and through

하나부터 열까지 literally means "from one to ten" and is often used together with words like 알다 (= to know), 설명하다 (= to explain), and 신경쓰다 (= to mind, to care about).

Ex)

내가 하나부터 열까지 다 설명해 줘야 돼?

= Do I have to explain everything in detail?

10. 하나를 보면 열을 알다

= you see one and you have seen them all

When you see one aspect of something or someone, you can often tell what the whole picture must be like. For example, when you see someone being rude to their friends, you can guess that they will also be rude to other people, including yourself. You can use this expression in these types of situations. When you want to link this expression with other phrases, you can start your sentence with 하나를 보면 열을 알 수 있다는데 (= they say that you can see what someone is like from one behavior, and...), or 하나를 보면 열을 안다고 (= like the saying "you see one and you know ten").

Ex)

하나를 보면 열을 알 수 있다는데, 여기서 이렇게 행동하면, 집에서는 어떻겠어요?

= They say that if you see one you can know ten, and if he behaves like this here, what will he be like at home?

Track 51

Sample Dialogue

보람: 이게 다 뭐예요? 이사 가니까 다
　　　버리려고요?

두루: 네.

보람: 하나도 남김없이 다요? 아깝다. 만에 하나
　　　나중에 다시 필요하면 어떡해요?

두루: 필요 없을 것 같아요. 필요하면 다시
　　　사야겠죠.

*Boram: What's all this? Are you going to throw
away all of this since you are moving?*

Duru: Yes.

*Boram: All of it? It's a waste! I know it is unlikely,
but what if you need it again later on?*

*Duru: I don't think I will need it. If I need it, I guess
I'll just buy it again.*

✎ Exercises for Lesson **26**

Fill in the blanks with the appropriate idioms with 하나 from this lesson.

1. (   )

   = to not hurt at all

2. (   )

   = from A to Z, every little detail, through and through

3. (   )

   = by any possibility, out of a low probability

4. (   )

   = without leaving anything, without anything left over, completely

5. (   )

   = you see one and you have seen them all

Check the answers on **p. 234**

LESSON **27**

Showing Empathy or Shock

> # 얼마나 -(으)ㄹ까(요), 얼마나 -(으)면

When asking about the amount or degree of something, you can use the word 얼마나 to say things like "how big (얼마나 큰)", "how fast (얼마나 빠른)", and "how high (얼마나 높은)". In this lesson, we are going to look at two useful expressions that use 얼마나.

I. 얼마나 -(으)ㄹ까(요)

얼마나 means "how much" or "to what extent", and -(으)ㄹ까(요) expresses a guess or assumption. All together, "얼마나 + verb stem + -(으)ㄹ까(요)" means "how ... will it be?"

Ex)
저 건물은 얼마나 비쌀까(요)?

= How expensive will that building over there be?

= I wonder how expensive that building over there is.

You can express empathy by imagining the other person's situation by using "얼마나 -(으)ㄹ까(요)" with a word related to one's feelings, such as 좋다, 아프다, 힘들다, 속상하다, 기쁘다, etc. In this case, the expression is often followed by 생각하니(까) to mean "thinking about how much/to what extent one must have done so-and-so". If you are talking about an incident in the past, you can use "얼마나 -았/었/였을까(요)".

"얼마나 -(으)ㄹ까(요)" is also often used when you are thinking out loud, and not necessarily expecting an answer. When used in this way, you say it in 반말 without -요.

Track 53

Sample Sentences

얼마나 좋을까?

= How good would it be?

= How happy he must be!

얼마나 아플까요?

= How painful would it be?

= How painful it must be!

얼마나 아팠을까?

= I wonder how painful it must have been.

= I wonder how painful it was.

얼마나 힘들었을까요?

= I wonder how hard it must have been.

= I wonder how hard it was.

그 사람이 얼마나 힘들었을까 생각하니 가슴이 아파요.

= It breaks my heart to think about how much he must have suffered.

제 친구들이 얼마나 고생했을까 생각하니 미안하네요.

= I feel bad thinking about how much work it must have been for my friends.

2. 얼마나 -(으)면

얼마나 means "how much" and -(으)면 means "if". The actual meaning of this phrase is "in order for THAT to have happened, there must have been this much of THIS". The part before -(으)면 can be in the past tense, too, as in 얼마나 -았/었/였으면.

Examples

Track 53

얼마나 추웠으면 = how cold he must have been (in order for him to do that)

얼마나 바쁘면 = how busy she must be (in order for her to do that)

얼마나 맛있으면 = how tasty it must be (in order for that to happen)

얼마나 -(으)면 is usually paired with endings like -겠어(요)? or -(으)ㄹ까(요)?

얼마나 A + -(으)면 + B + -겠어(요)?

= How (much) A do you think it is for B to happen?

얼마나 A + -(으)면 + B + -(으)ㄹ까(요)?

= How (much) A do you think will it have to be for B to happen?

Sample Sentences

얼마나 무거웠으면 끈이 끊어졌을까?

= I wonder how heavy it must have been for the strap to have snapped.

얼마나 재미있었으면 게임을 열 시간 동안 했을까?

= I wonder how fun it was for them to play the video game for 10 hours.

= The game must have been a lot of fun because they played it for 10 hours.

얼마나 노래를 불렀으면 목이 저렇게 쉬었을까요?

= I wonder how much she sang for her voice to get that hoarse.

얼마나 급했으면 선생님이 직접 전화했겠어요?

= How urgent must it have been for the teacher to have called in person?

얼마나 걱정됐으면 제가 여기까지 왔겠어요?

= Can you guess how worried I was to come all the way here?

= I was so worried that I came all the way here.

Track
53

Sample Dialogue

Track 54

현우: 석진 씨 결국 박사 과정 그만뒀대요.

경은: 정말요? 한 학기 남았는데... 얼마나 힘들었으면 그만뒀을까...

현우: 일하면서 공부하기 쉽지 않죠.

경은: 박사 과정 합격하고 정말 좋아했는데... 석진 씨가 얼마나 속상할까 생각하니 마음이 아프네요.

Hyunwoo: I heard that Seokjin quit doing his PhD in the end.

Kyeong-eun: Really? He had one semester left. How difficult it must have been for him to have just given up.

Hyunwoo: It's surely not easy to study while also working.

Kyeong-eun: He was so happy when he got accepted into the PhD program. My heart aches to think about how upset he must be.

✏️ *Exercises for Lesson* **27**

Check the answers on **p. 235**

Fill in the blanks using 얼마나 –(으)ㄹ까 *or* 얼마나 –(으)면.

1. (   ) 목이 저렇게 쉬었을까요?

   = I wonder how much she sang for her voice to get that hoarse.

2. (   ) 제가 여기까지 왔겠어요?

   = Can you guess how worried I was to come all the way here?

3. (   ) 선생님이 직접 전화했겠어요?

   = How urgent must it have been for the teacher to have called in person?

4. 그 사람이 (   ) 생각하니 가슴이 아파요.

   = It breaks my heart to think about how much he must have suffered.

5. 제 친구들이 (   ) 생각하니 미안하네요.

   = I feel bad thinking about how much work it must have been for my friends.

203

LESSON 28

싶다 Used to Mean "To think" or "To wonder"

-(으)ㄴ/는가 싶다, -나 싶다, -(으)ㄹ까 싶다

Track
55

In Level 1 Lesson 13, we introduced -고 싶다, which means "to want to". It is one of the most basic sentence endings in Korean and is probably quite familiar to you. But in addition to the form of "-고 싶다", 싶다 also has some other usages that are very interesting and useful to know.

In addition to meaning "to want to", 싶다 can also mean "to think", "to wonder", or "to be not sure if". It is used in the form of -(으)ㄴ/는가 싶다, -나 싶다, or -(으)ㄹ까 싶다. When it is used in the sense of "to wonder", 싶다 often expresses the speaker's doubt about something being possible or true. The exact meaning of 싶다 really depends on the context of the conversation because even when used in the same sentence structure 싶다 can mean either "I think" or "I doubt".

1. Verb stem + -(으)ㄴ/는가 싶다

-(으)ㄴ/는가 싶다 is most commonly used in the form of 아닌가 싶다 and 건가 싶다.

건가 싶다 is the shortened form of 것인가 싶다. 아닌가 싶다 originally means "I wonder if it is not", and can be translated to "I think it is".

Sample Sentences

은희 씨요? 오늘 휴가가 아닌가 싶어요.

= Eunhee? I think she is off-duty today.

= **은희 씨요? 오늘 휴가인 것 같아요.**

옆집 사람들한테도 말해 줘야 하는 거 아닌가 싶어요.

= I think we need to tell our next-door neighbors, too.

= **옆집 사람들한테도 말해 줘야 할 것 같아요.**

둘이 같이 일하는 건가 싶었어요.

= I was wondering if they work together.

= **둘이 같이 일하는 건지 궁금했어요.**

Track 55

회의가 끝난 건가 싶어서 문을 열어 봤어요.

= I wondered if the meeting was over so I opened the door.

= **회의가 끝난 건지 궁금해서 문을 열어 봤어요.**

제 생각이 틀린 건가 싶어요.

= I feel like I might be wrong.

= **제 생각이 틀린 건지도 모르겠다는 생각이 들어요.**

2. Verb stem + -나 싶다

-나 싶다 can be thought of as a question to oneself in the form of "verb stem + -나?"

205

followed by 싶다, which means "I wonder" in this usage. Since you are questioning something, it means that you are not sure about it. This structure is often used in the form of -지 않나 싶다 as well. You can think of -지 않나 싶다 as "I ask myself ＋ isn't this so-and-so?", which can be translated to "I think".

Sample Sentences

이게 맞나 싶어요.

= I am not sure if this is correct.

= 이게 맞는지 모르겠어요.

이게 다 무슨 의미가 있나 싶어요.

= I do not know what this all means.

= 이게 다 무슨 의미가 있는지 모르겠어요.

사람들이 왜 이런 걸 좋아하나 싶어요.

= I wonder why people like this kind of stuff.

= 사람들이 왜 이런 걸 좋아하는지 모르겠어요.

왜 그런 말을 하나 싶었어요.

= I wondered why he/she said such a thing.

= 왜 그런 말을 하는 것인지 궁금했어요.

= 왜 그런 말을 하는 것인지 이해할 수 없었어요.

이건 초등학생에게는 너무 어렵지 않나 싶어요.

= I feel like this is too difficult for an elementary school student.

= 이건 초등학생에게는 너무 어려운 것 같아요.

어딘가에서 공사를 하고 있지 않나 싶어요.

= I guess they are doing construction somewhere.

= **어딘가에서 공사를 하고 있는 것 같아요.**

When talking about a past incident, you can add the past tense suffix -았/었/였-.

Ex)

이게 다 무슨 의미가 있었나 싶어요.

= I do not know what this all meant.

= I do not understand anymore why we did all that.

이건 초등학생에게는 너무 어렵지 않았나 싶어요.

= I feel like this was too difficult for an elementary school student.

Track 55

3. Verb stem + -(으)ㄹ까 싶다

-(으)ㄹ까 싶다 can be translated in a similar way to the two previous 싶다 expressions. Because -(으)ㄹ까 is in the future tense, it is commonly used to talk about a future possibility or your assumption about the future.

Sample Sentences

진짜 이게 다 필요할까 싶어요.

= I am not sure if all this will be really necessary.

= **진짜 이게 다 필요할지 모르겠어요.**

정말로 다 할 수 있을까 싶어요.

= I am not sure if we can really do all of this.

= **정말로 다 할 수 있을지 모르겠어요.**

어렵지 않을까 싶어요.

= I feel like this will be difficult.

= 어려울 것 같아요.

제가 직접 말하면 오해가 생기지 않을까 싶어요.

= I feel like there will be a misunderstanding if I talk to them directly.

= 제가 직접 말하면 오해가 생길 것 같아요.

Unlike -(으)ㄴ/는가 싶다 or -나 싶다, -(으)ㄹ까 싶다 can also be used when talking about what you are considering doing.

Sample Sentences

오늘은 그냥 집에 일찍 갈까 싶어요.

= I am thinking maybe I should just go home early today.

= 오늘은 그냥 집에 일찍 가려고 생각 중이에요.

저 혼자는 못 할 것 같아서 도움을 요청할까 싶어요.

= I do not think I will be able to do it by myself, so I am thinking of asking for help.

= 저 혼자는 못 할 것 같아서 도움을 요청할까 생각 중이에요.

Track
55

Sample Dialogue

Track 56

다혜: 화연 씨 왔어요?

은희: 아직요. 6시 넘어서 도착하지 않을까 싶어요.

다혜: 화연 씨랑 같이 이야기하는 게 낫지 않나 싶은데... 그럼 내일 화연 씨 있을 때 다시 이야기할까요?

은희: 좋아요. 그럼 내일 다시 이야기해요.

Dahye: Is Hwa-yeon here?

Eunhee: Not yet. I feel like she will arrive after six o'clock.

Dahye: I feel like it's better to talk about this with Hwa-yeon too. Shall we talk again tomorrow when Hwa-yeon is around?

Eunhee: Sounds good. Let's talk again tomorrow then.

✐ *Exercises for Lesson 28*

Rewrite the following sentences using -(으)ㄴ/는가 싶다, -나 싶다, *or* -(으)ㄹ까 싶다.

1. 이게 맞는지 모르겠어요.

→ ....

2. 어려울 것 같아요.

→ ....

3. 둘이 같이 일하는 건지 궁금했어요.

→ ....

4. 이게 다 무슨 의미가 있는지 모르겠어요.

→ ....

5. 회의가 끝난 건지 궁금해서 문을 열어 봤어요.

→ ....

6. 제가 직접 말하면 오해가 생길 것 같아요.

→ ....

LESSON 29

Double Negative = Positive

없지 않다, 없지 않아 있다

In this lesson, we are going to take a look at a unique way to make an affirmative sentence through a double negative. The expressions we will study are 없지 않다 and 없지 않아 있다. They have basically the same meaning and can be used interchangeably, so let us look mainly at 없지 않다 for now.

Track 57

없지 않다

없다 means "to not exist" and -지 않다 makes the sentence negative. So 없지 않다 translates to "it does not NOT exist" and therefore means "it does exist". This phrase is common in Korean because 없다 itself is a stand-alone verb, unlike in English where 없다 is only expressed through the negative form of 있다 (= to exist).

The structure of 없지 않다 is similar to the way 작지 않다 (= to be not small) is used to say, "It is big" or 쉽지 않다 (= to be not easy) is used to say, "It is difficult." Both 없지 않다 and 없지 않아 있다 can be used to say "있다" in a softer and more careful manner. The

211

expression is often used in the form of 없지 않죠 or 없지 않아 있죠 to express agreement with what someone has just said.

Examples

그런 경우가 없지 않아요.

= That does happen from time to time.

= There are such cases from time to time.

= 그런 경우가 가끔 있어요.

위험 요소가 없지 않죠.

= There is définitely some risk.

= There is a degree of risk.

= 위험 요소가 어느 정도 있죠.

* 위험 요소 = risk factor

Words commonly used together with 없지 않다

Some words are used frequently with the expressions 없지 않다 and 없지 않아 있다. 감 (feeling, sensation), 느낌 (sensation), 경우 (case), 경향 (tendency), 부분 (part), and 면 (aspect) are used often.

Verb stem + -(으)ㄴ/는 감이 없지 않다 = It does feel like...

Verb stem + -(으)ㄴ/는 느낌이 없지 않다 = It does feel like...

Verb stem + -(으)ㄴ/는 경우가 없지 않다 = There are certainly some cases where...

Verb stem + -(으)ㄴ/는 경향이 없지 않다 = There is some tendency to...

Verb stem + -(으)ㄴ/는 부분이 없지 않다 = There are some parts that...

Verb stem + -(으)ㄴ/는 면이 없지 않다 = There are some aspects where...

In addition to these words, the word 것 is also quite commonly used with 없지 않다 in the form of -(으)ㄴ/는 게 없지 않다. In this case, 것 is used as 게, which is the shortened form of 것이. 것 has the same meaning as 부분 (part) or 면 (aspect).

Another expression commonly used with 없지 않다 is 아무래도, which means "after much thought", "no matter what I try", or "I cannot deny". 아무래도 is used either at the beginning of the sentence, as in "아무래도 그런 면이 없지 않죠", or right before 없지 않다, as in "그런 면이 아무래도 없지 않죠."

Sample Sentences

그런 우려가 없지 않아 있죠.

= There is certainly such a concern.

= We do have that as a concern.

   * 우려 = concern

Track 57

좀 비싼 느낌이 없지 않죠.

= It does feel a bit expensive.

= I do feel like it is a bit expensive.

사업을 하다 보면 아무래도 손해를 보는 경우가 없지 않죠.

= As things are when running a business, there are certainly times when you have a deficit.

= While running a business, there are certainly instances where you lose money.

   * 손해를 보다 = to suffer a loss

그리고 사고가 날 가능성도 없지 않죠.

= And there is definitely the possibility that an accident will happen.

   * 가능성 = possibility

213

가족이랑 같은 직장에서 일하면 편한 부분도 없지 않아 있죠.

= If you work with a family member at the same workplace, there are certainly convenient aspects, too.

아무래도 그런 면도 없지 않죠.

= I cannot deny that there are those aspects, too.

솔직히 말하면 그런 게 없지 않죠.

= Honestly speaking, that is true to an extent.

= Honestly speaking, that does happen from time to time.

대기업에서는 일 처리 속도가 느린 면이 없지 않죠.

= At a large corporation, there is certainly the tendency for things to get done slowly.

  * 대기업 = large company, conglomerate

  ** 처리 = handling, processing

Sample Dialogue

Track
58

경화: 이 디자인이 좋기는 한데, 좀 평범한
　　　느낌이 없지 않아 있는 것 같아요.

보람: 음... 그래요?

경화: 여기에 그림을 하나 넣는 건 어떨까요?

보람: 여기에 그림이 들어가면 책 제목이 눈에
　　　잘 안 띌 거예요.

경화: 아, 그럴 가능성이 없지 않아 있겠네요.

* 평범하다 = *to be plain, to be run-of-the-mill*

Kyung-hwa: *I do like this design, but it does feel a*
　　　　　bit plain.

Boram: *Umm, you think so?*

Kyung-hwa: *What do you think of adding a*
　　　　　drawing here?

Boram: *If we add a drawing here, the book title*
　　　　　won't really stand out.

Kyung-hwa: *Ah, I guess there's the possibility that*
　　　　　it won't.

215

✎ Exercises for Lesson 29

Rewrite the following sentences using 없지 않다 *and* 없지 않아 있다.

1. 그런 우려가 어느 정도 있죠. = There is certainly such a concern.

    → ....

    → ....

2. 위험 요소가 어느 정도 있죠. = There is definitely some risk.

    → ....

    → ....

3. 아무래도 그런 면도 어느 정도 있죠. = I cannot deny that there are those aspects, too.

    → ....

    → ....

4. 사고가 날 가능성도 어느 정도 있죠. = There is definitely the possibility that an accident will happen.

    → ....

    → ....

5. 솔직히 말하면 그런 게 어느 정도 있죠. = Honestly speaking, that is true to an extent.

    → ....

    → ....

Check the answers on **p. 235**

LESSON **30**

Sentence Building Drill 20

Sentence Building Drill 20

In this series, we focus on how to use the grammatical rules and expressions that you have previously learned to train yourself to comfortably make Korean sentences.

Track
59

We will start off with THREE key sentences and practice changing different parts of these sentences so that you do not end up simply memorizing the same three sentences. We want you to be able to make Korean sentences as flexibly as possible.

Key Sentence (1)
급하게 일하다 보면 실수를 하기 마련이니까, 다시 한번 확인해야겠어요.
= When you work in a hurry, you are bound to make mistakes, so I am going to check again.

Key Sentence (2)
주연 씨가 얼마나 빨리 퇴근하고 싶었으면 이 일을 이렇게 빨리 끝냈나 싶어요.
= Jooyeon must have really wanted to leave the office early because she finished this work this fast.

217

Key Sentence (3)

지금 프로그램을 한꺼번에 여러 개 돌리고 있어서인지 컴퓨터가 좀 느려진 감이 없지 않아 있어요.

= Maybe because I am running several programs at the same time, it does feel like my computer has become a bit slow.

Expansion & Variation Practice with Key Sentence (1)

0. Original sentence:

급하게 일하다 보면 실수를 하기 마련이니까, 다시 한번 확인해야겠어요.

= When you work in a hurry, you are bound to make mistakes, so I am going to check again.

Track 59

1.

급하게 일하다 보면 실수를 하기 마련이니까

= When you work in a hurry, you are bound to make mistakes, so...

생방송을 처음 하다 보면 떨리기 마련이니까

= When you do a live show for the first time, you are bound to get nervous, so...

처음엔 누구나 실수를 하기 마련이에요.

= At first, everybody makes mistakes.

이런 일이 생기면 누구나 당황하기 마련이에요.

= When something like this happens, everybody panics.

외국어는 안 쓰면 잊어버리기 마련이에요.

= When you do not use a foreign language, you are bound to forget it.

2.

다시 한번 확인해야겠어요.

= I need to check again.

지금 전화해 봐야겠어요

= I need to call them now.

저도 내일부터 연습해야겠어요.

= I need to start practicing from tomorrow.

우리 내일은 더 일찍 와야겠어요.

= We will have to come here earlier tomorrow.

이거 말고 다른 걸로 사야겠어요.

= We will have to buy something else instead of this.

Expansion & Variation Practice with Key Sentence (2)

0. Original sentence:

주연 씨가 얼마나 빨리 퇴근하고 싶었으면 이 일을 이렇게 빨리 끝냈나 싶어요.

= Jooyeon must have really wanted to leave the office early because she finished this work this fast.

Track 59

I.

주연 씨가 얼마나 빨리 퇴근하고 싶었으면

= I wonder how badly Jooyeon wanted to leave the office early (for her to do this)

주연 씨가 얼마나 그 가방이* 사고 싶었으면

= I wonder how badly Jooyeon wanted to buy that bag (for her to do this)

아이들이 아이스크림이* 얼마나 먹고 싶었으면

= I wonder how badly the kids wanted to eat ice cream (for them to do this)

밖이 얼마나 추웠으면

= I wonder how cold it was outside (for this to happen)

책을 얼마나 많이 샀으면

= I wonder how many books they bought (for this to happen)

* The -이 particle in 가방이 and 아이스크림이 are auxiliary particles, not subject marking particles. Auxiliary particles are often attached after the object in a sentence that uses the expression -고 싶다. This is because auxiliary particles put more emphasis on how much you would like to do something, compared to using -을/를 with -고 싶다.

2.
얼마나 빨리 퇴근하고 싶었으면 이 일을 이렇게 빨리 끝냈나 싶어요.
= I wonder how badly she wanted to leave the office early for her to have finished this work so quickly.
어떻게 거기에서 10년 동안 살았나 싶어요.
= I wonder how I lived there for 10 years.
언제 애들이 이렇게 컸나 싶어요.
= I wonder when the kids grew so much like this.
이 두꺼운 책을 언제 다 읽나 싶어요.
= I wonder when I can read this thick book.
집 청소를 언제 다 하나 싶어요.
= I wonder when I can finish cleaning the house.

Expansion & Variation Practice with Key Sentence (3)

0. Original sentence:
지금 프로그램을 한꺼번에 여러 개 돌리고 있어서인지 컴퓨터가 좀 느려진 감이 없지 않아 있어요.
= Maybe because I am running several programs at the same time, it does feel like my computer has become a bit slow.

1.

지금 프로그램을 한꺼번에 여러 개 돌리고 있어서인지

= maybe because I am running several programs at the same time

날씨가 계속 더워서인지

= maybe because the weather keeps being hot

하루 종일 걸어서인지

= maybe because I walked all day long

쉬는 시간 없이 계속 일해서 그런지

= maybe because I kept working without taking a break

낮에 커피를 네 잔이나 마셔서인지

= maybe because I had four cups of coffee during the day

2.

컴퓨터가 좀 느려진 감이 없지 않아 있어요.

= It does feel like my computer has become a bit slow.

다른 방보다 어두운 감이 없지 않아요.

= It does feel like it is darker than the other rooms.

아직은 좀 이른 감이 없지 않죠.

= It does feel like it is a little too early (to do that) now.

지금 사과하기에는 좀 늦은 감이 없지 않죠.

= It does feel like it is a little late for an apology.

행사가 취소될 가능성도 없지 않아요.

= There certainly is a possibility that the event might be canceled.

Track
59

Sample Dialogue

Track
60

동근: 낮잠을 자서 그런지 잠이 안 오네요.

경은: 낮잠 자면 밤에 잠 안 온다고, 제가 낮잠
　　　자지 말라고 했잖아요.

동근: 경은 씨 말 들을걸. 잠이 올 때까지
　　　텔레비전 좀 봐야겠어요.

경은: 텔레비전 보면 잠이 더 안 올걸요?
　　　차라리 책을 읽는 건 어때요?

동근: 책이라는 말만 들어도 벌써 졸리네요.

Dong-geun: Maybe because I took a nap, I can't sleep.

Kyeong-eun: I told you not to take a nap because you
　　　　　　won't be able to sleep at night if you do.

Dong-geun: I should have listened to you. I guess I
　　　　　　should watch TV until I get sleepy.

Kyeong-eun: You'll probably be even less sleepy if you
　　　　　　watch TV. How about reading a book
　　　　　　instead?

Dong-geun: I'm already sleepy just hearing the word
　　　　　　"book".

✏ Exercises for Lesson **30**

Using what you learned in Talk To Me In Korean Level 10, fill in the blanks to match the English translation.

1. 쉬는 시간 없이 계속 일해서 ☐☐☐

= maybe because I kept working without taking a break

2. 주연 씨가 ☐☐☐ 빨리 퇴근하고 싶었으면

= I wonder how badly Jooyeon wanted to leave the office early (for her to do this).

3. 저도 내일부터 연습해야 ☐☐☐.

= I need to start practicing from tomorrow.

4. 언제 애들이 이렇게 컸나 ☐☐☐.

= I wonder when the kids grew so much like this.

5. 행사가 취소될 가능성도 ☐☐ 않아요.

= There certainly is a possibility that the event might be canceled.

6. 외국어는 안 쓰면 잊어버리기 ☐☐ 이에요.

= When you do not use a foreign language, you are bound to forget it.

Check the answers on **P. 235**

BLOG

Island Life vs. City Life

I have lived in Korea for a little over ten years, and I have spent most of that time in Korea's biggest city, Seoul. I met my wife on my first trip to Jeju Island, an island off the southern coast of Korea. I immediately fell in love with both the person I met and the island itself. Throughout our relationship, we visited Jeju several times throughout the year. Then, a few years ago, we decided to give up city life and head down to make a home on this beautiful island. Now, when moving to an island from a city, there are a few things you should keep in mind. In this blog, my goal is to hopefully provide some insight about what it is like to live on an island versus in a city.

Slow Down

Before moving to Jeju, many of my Korean friends expressed their concern about the challenges of adapting to the much slower lifestyle on the island. I even heard stories about people who moved to Jeju only to move back to Seoul a year or so later. One of the reasons was that they could not adjust to the slower pace of how things work. I get it – once you get accustomed to the fast lifestyle of a city, it can be daunting and hard to get used to things moving at a much slower speed. This has not been a challenge for me, however, as I tend to like things moving slower. I like taking time out of my day to just take little moments here and there to take in and appreciate what I have. I feel like some of that gets lost in the hustle and bustle of city life. So, if you do plan on moving to an island, be prepared to slow things down.

Public Transportation

One of the biggest differences between living on an island and living in a city is the public transportation. If you do not have a car, you can certainly get around the island. There are buses that will take you just about anywhere, and when there isn't a bus, you can take a taxi, which are relatively cheap here in Korea. However, the amount of time you will spend waiting for and riding buses is a bit more than you might be used to. If you are used to how things work in Seoul, this can be a bit frustrating. In Seoul, you have a few different options for transportation, including buses and subways. If you miss a bus in Seoul, it is typically not a problem because another bus will always come in a couple of minutes. However, this is not always the case on Jeju. There is no subway system, and if you miss a bus, you may have to wait up to 30 minutes for the next one. So, when you do things using public transportation, you really have to plan out your trip, even if it is just to head over to the store to buy some groceries.

Winters can be Cold

One thing people may expect is that they can leave
the bitter cold winters of Seoul and head down to
one of Korea's islands for a warmer lifestyle. While
it might be a bit warmer during the summer, it also
gets quite cold during the winter. In fact, it even
snows on some of the islands, especially in areas
with high elevation. One of the reasons it gets so
cold is due to the wind coming in from the ocean.
The wind is strong and will cut through just about
any layer of clothing you have on, so be sure to
bundle up. And since we are talking about weather,
one thing to know is the drastic weather change
you can see on the same day. For instance, my wife
and I visited one side of the island, and when we got
there, it was cool, windy, and overcast. It even began

to rain so we decided to cut our trip short and find some shelter from the rain. After having
lunch, we drove back to our home in Jeju City, where we found it hot and quite sunny. This
is quite typical for the island, so if you are visiting, it is a good idea to bring a light jacket even
during some of the warmer seasons. Even in summer it can get a bit cool at night. This kind
of change in weather that varies by region is not something you will see a lot of in a city like
Seoul. Typically, if it is hot in one area, it is going to be hot everywhere.

Entertainment

One of the best things about living in a big city is the amount of entertainment you have at
your fingertips. However, that is not always the case on an island. Sure, you can go swimming

or surfing in the ocean, but what do you do when it is too cold to go into the water? If you are like me and enjoy watching movies at the theater, you may not have much to choose from. Jeju City has a few theaters, but one thing I miss is watching some of the big blockbuster movies on IMAX. There still is no IMAX theater on the island, so we just have to settle for normal theaters. In Seoul, there are all kinds of theaters to try out, but we are a bit limited here in

Jeju. However, because there is more space on the island, there are also more opportunities for unique theaters like a drive-in theater, which Jeju Island does have. This theater is neat because you can watch a movie on the big screen from your car. That means you get to watch movies like they did in the past. Plus, you get to control the air-conditioning.

To sum it up, neither city life nor island life is better than the other. They both have their own unique qualities. It really depends on what you like. Which leads me to ask you the following: which do you prefer? Do you like the busy streets of the city, or would you rather slow down and soak up the scenery of an island?

Written by Johnny Bland

Level 10을 모두 끝냈어요*!*
정말 축하합니다*!!*

ANSWERS

for Level 10, Lessons 1 ~ 30

Answers for Level 10, Lesson 1

1. 얼굴에 철판을 깔다

2. 얼굴만 내밀다

3. 얼굴에 쓰여 있다

4. 얼굴을 붉히다

5. 얼굴이 좋아 보이다

Answers for Level 10, Lesson 2

1. 옷 찾으러 왔어요.

2. 수영하러 갈래요?

3. 잠깐 인사하러 왔어요.

4. 석진 씨요? 운동하러 갔어요.

5. 여기가 제가 피아노 배우러 가는 곳이에요.

Answers for Level 10, Lesson 3

1. 아무리 그렇다지만, 이건 너무했네요.

2. 아무리 가족이라지만, 이해할 수 없어요.

3. 아무리 가까운 친구라지만, 돈을 허락 없이 쓰면 안 돼요.

4. 아무리 잘 먹는다지만, 어떻게 피자 세 판을 먹어요?

5. 아무리 바쁘다지만, 전화는 할 수 있잖아요?

Answers for Level 10, Lesson 4

1. 라도

2. 나

3. 나

4. 라도

5. 라도

6. 나

7. 나

8. 라도

Answers for Level 10, Lesson 5

1. 안 하기로 하지 않았어요

2. 만나기로 했어요

3. 계획 먼저 세우기로 해요

4. 여기서 만나기로 해요

5. 10시에 만나기로 했는데

Answers for Level 10, Lesson 6

1. 되는 일이 없다

2. 볼일

3. 일이 산더미처럼 쌓여 있다

4. 일이 손에 안 잡히다

5. 일이 잘 풀리다

Answers for Level 10, Lesson 7

1. ②

2. ②

3. ①

4. 다거나

5. 다거나

Answers for Level 10, Lesson 8

1. 앉은 채로 or 앉아 있는 채로

2. 신은 채로 or 신고 있는 채로

3. 든 채로 or 들고 있는 채로

4. 모르는 채로 (모른 채로 is grammatically incorrect, but is often used colloquially.)

5. 입은 채로 or 입고 있는 채로

Answers for Level 10, Lesson 9

1. ③

2. ①

3. ②

4. ③

5. ③

Answers for Level 10, Lesson 10

1. 항상, 편

2. 아무리

3. 원래, 기로

4. 간다거나 할 때는

5. 산더미

Answers for Level 10, Lesson 11

1. 비쌀 텐데

2. 좋을 텐데

3. 바쁠 텐데

4. 재밌을 텐데 or 재미있을 텐데

5. 수영했을 텐데

Answers for Level 10, Lesson 12

1. ②

2. ①

3. ②

4. ②

5. ②

Answers for Level 10, Lesson 13

1. 제 친구가 사람들한테 다 말해서, 모두 도와서 일을 빨리 끝냈어요. (= My friend told everyone, so everybody helped and we finished the work early.)

   제 친구가 사람들한테 다 말하는 바람에, 우리 비밀 계획을 모두 알게 됐어요. (= As a result of my friend telling everyone, they all found out about our secret plan.)

2. 컴퓨터가 갑자기 고장 나서 새 컴퓨터를 샀어요. (= My computer suddenly broke down, so I bought a new one.)

   컴퓨터가 갑자기 고장 나는 바람에 숙제가 다 지워졌어요. (= My computer suddenly broke down, so my homework got deleted.)

3. 지갑을 집에 놓고 와서 다혜 씨한테 얻어먹었어요. (= I left my wallet at home, so Dahye bought my meal.)

   지갑을 집에 놓고 오는 바람에 선물을 못 샀어요. (= I left my wallet at home, so I could not buy a present.)

4. 갑자기 친구가 들어와서 깜짝 놀랐지만 반가웠어요. (= My friend suddenly came in and I was really surprised, but glad to see her/him.)

   갑자기 친구가 들어오는 바람에 다 들켰어요. (= My friend suddenly came in, and I got caught completely.)

5. 오늘 아침에 늦게 일어나서 안 피곤해요. (= I got up late this morning, so I am not tired.)

   오늘 아침에 늦게 일어나는 바람에 수업에 지각했어요. (= I got up late this morning, so I was late for class.)

Answers for Level 10, Lesson 14

1. ①

2. ①

3. ②

4. ②

5. ②

Answers for Level 10, Lesson 15

1. 꼬마야, 넌 이름이 뭐니?

2. 너는 왜 우니?

3. 여기서 혼자 뭐 하니?

4. 너 제정신이니?

5. 나 왜 이렇게 멍청하니?

Answers for Level 10, Lesson 16

1. 비 안 맞게 조심하세요.

2. 멀리서도 볼 수 있게 크게 써 주세요.

3. 모두 다 들을 수 있게 큰 소리로 말해 주세요.

4. 넘어지지 않게 조심하세요.

5. 마감 기한을 지킬 수 있게 미리 준비해 주세요.

Answers for Level 10, Lesson 17

1. 일이라기보다는

2. 먹는다기보다는

3. 어렵다기보다는

4. 싫다기보다는

5. 탄다기보다는

Answers for Level 10, Lesson 18

1. 돈이 남기는커녕 모자랐어요.

2. 숙제를 다 하기는커녕 시작조차 못 했어요.

3. 저는 해외는커녕 서울 밖에도 안 나가 봤어요.

4. 칭찬받기는커녕 야단만 맞았어요.

5. 제 여동생은 주말에 집안일을 돕기는커녕, 거의 집에 있지도 않아요.

Answers for Level 10, Lesson 19

1. 해서라도

2. 수를

3. 짓을

4. 내서라도

5. 새워서라도

6. 뒤져서라도

Answers for Level 10, Lesson 20

1. ④

2. ③

3. ①

Answers for Level 10, Lesson 21

1. 입에 발린 말을 하다

2. 말을 높이다

3. 말을 꺼내다

4. 말이 통하다

5. 말을 아끼다

Answers for Level 10, Lesson 22

1. 꺼내며

2. 웃으며

3. 빠르며

4. 좋으며

5. 식탁이며 의자며

6. 책이며 공책이며

Answers for Level 10, Lesson 23

1. 살이 좀 빠져서인지 더 젊어 보여요. (더 어려 보여요 is also possible.)

2. 오늘 커피를 너무 많이 마셔서인지 잠이 잘 안 와요.

3. 날씨가 좋아서인지 바닷가에 가고 싶어졌어요. (바다에 is also possible.)

4. 바람이 많이 불어서인지 어제보다 추운 것 같아요.

5. 제가 어제 잠을 많이 못 자서인지 오늘은 공부에 집중이 안 돼요.

Answers for Level 10, Lesson 24

1. 우리도 서둘러야겠어요.

2. 차 막히기 전에 출발해야겠어요.

3. 이제 플라스틱 빨대를 쓰지 말아야겠어요.

4. 이제 집에 가야겠다.

5. 나중에 먹어야겠다.

6. 밤늦게 뭘 먹지 말아야겠다.

Answers for Level 10, Lesson 25

1. 축구를 하다 보면 다치기 마련이에요.

2. 시간이 지나면 잊혀지기 마련이에요.

3. 공부는 정말 필요하면 열심히 하기 마련이에요.

4. 아무리 게을러도, 손님이 오면 집 청소를 하기 마련이에요.

6. 영원한 비밀은 없어요. 사람들이 다 알기 마련이에요.

7. 재미있게 공부하면 성적도 좋아지기 마련이에요.

* The sentences that are not found in this lesson are from Level 7, Lesson 25, which is about -게 되어 있다.

Answers for Level 10, Lesson 26

1. 하나도 안 아프다

2. 하나부터 열까지

3. 만에 하나

4. 하나도 남김없이

5. 하나를 보면 열을 알다

1. 얼마나 노래를 불렀으면

2. 얼마나 걱정됐으면

3. 얼마나 급했으면

4. 얼마나 힘들었을까

5. 얼마나 고생했을까

1. 이게 맞나 싶어요.

2. 어렵지 않을까 싶어요.

3. 둘이 같이 일하는 건가 싶었어요.

4. 이게 다 무슨 의미가 있나 싶어요.

5. 회의가 끝난 건가 싶어서 문을 열어 봤어요.

6. 제가 직접 말하면 오해가 생기지 않을까 싶어요.

1. 그런 우려가 없지 않죠.
   그런 우려가 없지 않아 있죠.

2. 위험 요소가 없지 않죠.
   위험 요소가 없지 않아 있죠.

3. 아무래도 그런 면도 없지 않죠.
   아무래도 그런 면도 없지 않아 있죠.

4. 사고가 날 가능성도 없지 않죠.
   사고가 날 가능성도 없지 않아 있죠.

5. 솔직히 말하면 그런 게 없지 않죠.
   솔직히 말하면 그런 게 없지 않아 있죠.

1. 그런지

2. 얼마나

3. 겠어요

4. 싶어요

5. 없지

6. 마련

Notes On Using This Book

Colored Text
Colored text indicates that there is an accompanying audio file. You can download the MP3 audio files at **https://talktomeinkorean.com/audio**.

Hyphen
Some grammar points have a hyphen attached at the beginning, such as -이/가, -(으)ㄹ 거예요, -(으)려고 하다, and -은/는커녕. This means that the grammar point is dependent, so it needs to be attached to another word such as a noun, a verb, or a particle.

Parentheses
When a grammar point includes parentheses, such as -(으)ㄹ 거예요 or (이)랑, this means that the part in the parentheses can be omitted depending on the word it is attached to.

Slash
When a grammar point has a slash, such as -아/어/여서 or -은/는커녕, this means that only one of the syllables before or after the slash can be used at a time. In other words, -은/는커녕 is used as either -은커녕 or -는커녕, depending on the word it is attached to.

Descriptive Verb
In TTMIK lessons, adjectives in English are referred to as "descriptive verbs" because they can be conjugated as verbs depending on the tense.